CAMBRIDGE LIBRARY COLLECTION

Books of enduring scholarly value

Anthropology

The first use of the word 'anthropology' in English was recorded in 1593, but its modern use to indicate the study and science of humanity became current in the late nineteenth century. At that time a separate discipline had begun to evolve from many component strands (including history, archaeology, linguistics, biology and anatomy), and the study of so-called 'primitive' peoples was given impetus not only by the reports of individual explorers but also by the need of colonial powers to define and classify the unfamiliar populations which they governed. From the ethnographic writings of early explorers to the 1898 Cambridge expedition to the Torres Straits, often regarded as the first truly 'anthropological' field research, these books provide eye-witness information on often vanished peoples and ways of life, as well as evidence for the development of a new scientific discipline.

The Races of Man and Their Distribution

The Cambridge anthropological expedition of 1898–9 to the Torres Strait and New Guinea, led by the zoologist and anthropologist Alfred Cort Haddon (1855–1940), marked an epoch in field methodology. This edition, published in 1924, examines some of the major physical differences between human beings that Haddon used to distinguish race, looking at skin colour, hair, stature, nose, face, and head form, and is thorough and wide-ranging in offering examples from throughout the world. He also suggests some reasons for the geographical distribution of the races. This was a new approach, though Haddon's findings are necessarily condensed here, providing a valuable work of reference rather than a full study. Forming the basis for a larger work, this book is is an important example of early scientific anthropology, while Haddon's curatorial work in the Museum of Archaeology and Ethnology in Cambridge made this a primary centre for anthropological study and research.

T0345413

Cambridge University Press has long been a pioneer in the reissuing of out-of-print titles from its own backlist, producing digital reprints of books that are still sought after by scholars and students but could not be reprinted economically using traditional technology. The Cambridge Library Collection extends this activity to a wider range of books which are still of importance to researchers and professionals, either for the source material they contain, or as landmarks in the history of their academic discipline.

Drawing from the world-renowned collections in the Cambridge University Library and other partner libraries, and guided by the advice of experts in each subject area, Cambridge University Press is using state-of-the-art scanning machines in its own Printing House to capture the content of each book selected for inclusion. The files are processed to give a consistently clear, crisp image, and the books finished to the high quality standard for which the Press is recognised around the world. The latest print-on-demand technology ensures that the books will remain available indefinitely, and that orders for single or multiple copies can quickly be supplied.

The Cambridge Library Collection brings back to life books of enduring scholarly value (including out-of-copyright works originally issued by other publishers) across a wide range of disciplines in the humanities and social sciences and in science and technology.

The Races of Man and Their Distribution

ALFRED CORT HADDON

CAMBRIDGE UNIVERSITY PRESS

Cambridge, New York, Melbourne, Madrid, Cape Town,
Singapore, São Paolo, Delhi, Mexico City

Published in the United States of America by Cambridge University Press, New York

www.cambridge.org
Information on this title: www.cambridge.org/9781108046275

© in this compilation Cambridge University Press 2012

This edition first published 1909
This digitally printed version 2012

ISBN 978-1-108-04627-5 Paperback

This book reproduces the text of the original edition. The content and language reflect
the beliefs, practices and terminology of their time, and have not been updated.

Cambridge University Press wishes to make clear that the book, unless originally published
by Cambridge, is not being republished by, in association or collaboration with, or
with the endorsement or approval of, the original publisher or its successors in title.

The Races of Man.

JICARILLA APACHE

Races of Man

THE

RACES OF MAN

And Their Distribution

BY

A. C. HADDON, Sc.D., F.R.S.,

UNIVERSITY READER IN ETHNOLOGY,
CAMBRIDGE.

𝔌llustrated

LONDON

MILNER & COMPANY LIMITED, PATERNOSTER ROW,

AND RAGLAN WORKS, HALIFAX.

CONTENTS

LIST OF PLATES.

———oo🙰oo———

vii.

Plates I, IV, VIII, IX and X are from photographs taken at the St. Louis Exposition, 1904, by the staff of the Field Museum of Natural History, Chicago, and given to me by my friend, Dr. G. A. Dorsey, with full permission to reproduce them.

Plate II is from a photograph taken on the Cambridge Expedition to Torres Straits, etc., 1898.

Plates III, VI, and VII are from purchased photographs.

Plate V is from a photograph taken by my friend, Mr. J. Thomson.

INTRODUCTION

—➤◦◦—

IT is an extremely difficult matter to give in a very short space a well-balanced account of the races and peoples of mankind, for it is impossible to deal adequately with the subject in a small book ; and, furthermore, our information is far from complete. The present effort must necessarily be open to grave criticism from many standpoints.

This little work falls naturally into two parts. The first deals with some of the physical characters employed in classification, and a grouping of the main stocks according to those characters, together with their geographical distribution. The effects of European colonisation are entirely omitted.

The second part is devoted to a consideration of the five large areas, Oceania, Africa, Europe, Asia, and America. Each section is preceded by a sketch of the distribution of the races and peoples in the area, and a hypothetical sketch of some of the larger movements of population that may have taken place. Then follows a brief account of some of the more interesting peoples of that area. The selection was not easy, and perhaps too

much space has been given to the more backward
peoples, but the difficulty of dealing in a satisfactory
manner with the cultured peoples is very great, and the
reader can find detailed information in more ambitious
works. It will be noted that the treatment of Europe
is very different from that accorded to the other
continents, as it was felt that a statement of racial
elements in the population would be more generally
useful than an imperfect summary of national
characteristics.

Those who wish to advance further in this study
should consult Professor A. H. Keane's " Man, Past and
Present," "Ethnology," and "The World's Peoples";
Dr. J. Deniker's "The Races of Man"; and Professor
F. Ratzel's "The History of Mankind" (English
translation).

The omission of references is rightly open to serious
criticism, but it was felt that they would have to be so
numerous as to unduly increase the size of the book.
The short Bibliography at the end will, however, indicate
to the serious student some of the more important books
to consult.

Nearly all the special terms employed are explained
in the text on their first occurrence, but for the
convenience of the reader a short Glossary has been
added.

The Races of Man.

———∘∘⋋⊗⋌∘∘———

THE BASIS OF CLASSIFICATION

VARIOUS methods are employed in the attempt to group together different human communities and to distinguish between the races of mankind: these may be briefly described as physical, cultural and linguistic. The fact that languages may be readily borrowed by one people from another, renders linguistics unsatisfactory as a basis for classification. It certainly proves the contact of peoples, but does not necessarily imply racial affinity. We must therefore rank it as a subsidiary method. A classification based on culture may be of interest to the sociologist, but it is obviously one which can have no prime importance in regard to genetic relationship, though it may indicate the influence of peoples upon one another. There remain, therefore, the physical characters of different peoples upon which, as a foundation, a classification of mankind can most satisfactorily be erected.

The physical characters which can be employed in the grouping or discrimination of peoples are mainly of two kinds; those which are readily apparent, and those which require more minute observation, usually with the assistance of instruments. The most obvious of the superficial characters, such as stature, skin-colour, character of the hair, shape of the nose, and the like, have been recognised from time immemorial. Practically all peoples look upon their own physical characters as constituting the normal type, and consequently regard those that differ from them as being strange, and even repulsive. This is

1

proved by the frequency with which a people will class itself by a name which signifies "men," thereby implying that they only are men, while other peoples are designated by them under nicknames, names of localities, or of some peculiar habit.

SKIN-COLOUR.—Very obvious is the colour of the skin. Among the ancient Egyptians, the artists who decorated the royal tombs at Thebes (xix. dynasty) distinguished between four races:—(1) the Egyptians, whom they painted red; (2) the Asiatics or Semites, who were coloured yellow; (3) the Southerns or Negroes, who were naturally painted black; and (4) the Westerns or Northerns, white. We ourselves speak loosely of white men, yellow men, black men or "niggers," red men, and so forth. The coloration of the skin is a character of some importance, but we do not know accurately to what extent it can in time be influenced by climatic or other conditions. In the north of Europe we certainly do find a fair-skinned population, but the Greenland Eskimo has a brownish-yellow complexion, generally tinged with red. The very dark Negro of the equatorial forest does not appear to live under conditions very different from those of the pale yellow Punan of Borneo, nor are the conditions of existence dissimilar for the dark Fijian and the relatively fair Samoan. It does not seem possible at present to distinguish the relative importance of race and environment with regard to pigmentation. Perhaps when once fixed, pigmentation is a fairly constant character.

HAIR.—On the whole, the hair appears to be the most useful character in classifying the main groups of mankind. Practically everywhere outside Europe and parts of Northern Asia the hair is black in colour, often with a reddish, brownish, or bluish tinge. In Europe we have the greatest diversity, not only in colour, but in character. The three main varieties of hair are the straight, wavy, and so-called woolly. The first is lank hair that usually falls straight down, occasionally with a tendency to become wavy; it is apt to be coarse in texture. The second is undulating, or may form a long curve or imperfect spiral from one end to the other, or may be rolled spirally to form clustering rings or curls a centimetre ($\frac{3}{8}$ in.) or more in diameter. The third variety is characterised by numerous, close, often interlocking, spirals 1—9 mm. in diameter. These three varieties are now termed leiotrichous, cymotrichous, and ulotrichous. It must be remembered, however, that all intermediate conditions occur between these three types.

STATURE.—A commonly recognised distinction is that of stature; but though it is true that there are certain peoples who can be described as tall, medium, and short, or even as pygmy, the stature is apt to be very variable within certain limits among the same people. The average human stature appears to be about 1·675 m. (5ft. 6in.). Those peoples who are 1·725 m. (5ft. 8in.) or more in height are said to be tall; those below 1·625 m. (5ft. 4in.) are short, while those who fall below 1·500 m. (4ft. 11in.) are now usually termed pygmies.

NOSE.—A feature that has always attracted attention is the nose. It may be prominent or flat, and relatively to its length (i.e. from the root to the angle with the lip) the wings may be broad (platyrrhine), moderate (mesorrhine), or narrow (leptorrhine).

We have an interesting example of the employment of the above characters as a means of race discrimination in the Vedas, which were composed by the poets of the Aryan invaders of Northern India about 1500 B.C. The word *varna*, which is now employed to signify caste, is used in the dual number, "two colours," being the white of the Aryans and the black of the Dasyus, that is, of the Dravidian aborigines, who are elsewhere called "noseless," "black-skinned," "unholy," "excommunicated"; other texts dwell on their low stature, coarse features, and their voracious appetite. It is hardly an exaggeration to say that from these sources there might be compiled a fairly accurate anthropological definition of certain Dravidian tribes of to-day.

FACE.—The lower part of the face may project considerably (prognathous)—this is what is termed a "low" feature, or there may be no projection of the face (orthognathous). These characters are dependent on the size of the jaws. A flat and retreating forehead is also a "low" feature, but a somewhat bulbous forehead such as is characteristic of Negroes does not necessarily imply high intellectual ability. A straight nose, and one in which the root is only slightly marked, so that the line of the forehead passes gently into that of the nose, constitutes the classical nose of Greek statues. As a matter of fact, this feature was seized upon and exaggerated by certain Greek sculptors, the contours of the nose and forehead being alike falsified, so as to give increased nobility to the expression. The majesty of the brow of Zeus, the wielder of the destinies of men, was due to an overstepping of human contours, as these in their turn, in the dim ages of the past, had passed beyond the low outline of the brute.

HEAD-FORM.—Less obvious is the shape of the head. Looked at from above, some heads are distinctly narrow, while others are very broad. The nature of the hair and the fashion of dressing it often tend to obscure this, so for a satisfactory description recourse must be had to measurements. The measurements are rarely used by themselves, but are employed to give a ratio of the breadth to the length, the latter being taken at 100. Thus those heads in which the ratio of the breadth of the skull to its length falls below 75 are termed dolichocephalic or narrow-headed, those between 75 and 80 mesaticephalic or medium-headed, those exceeding 80 brachycephalic or broad-headed. Frequently only two groups are recognised, the dolichocephalic —78, and the brachycephalic 78+. When dealing with the skull only, it is better to speak of the cranial index, and to reserve the term cephalic index for the head of the living; roughly speaking, the cephalic index is two units higher than the cranial index. The height of the head is a character of some importance; some heads are high and well curved, while others are low and flattened.

There are many other characters which are employed by physical anthropologists which necessitate careful measurements on the living or on the skeleton, and the observation of certain details of anatomical structure; for these the reader is referred to special works dealing with physical anthropology.

Although, as a matter of convenience, the range of the variations of any given feature is divided up into groups to which definite names are applied, it must be clearly understood that these demarcations are perfectly arbitrary, and are employed merely to facilitate comparison and classification. Man is a very variable animal, and being able to travel long distances, a considerable mixture between different peoples has taken place; hence it becomes extremely difficult in some cases to determine whether the given modifications from the average type are due to the inherent variability of man, to reaction to the conditions under which he is living or has recently lived, or to actual race-mixture. These considerations necessitate caution in forming an opinion concerning the affinities of any people, and at the same time they demonstrate the extreme difficulty there is in framing a consistent classification of mankind.

Unfortunately there is a lack of uniformity in the employment of terms such as race, tribe, and for the minor divisions of a community, nor does it seem possible at the present time to bring all observers on these topics into line. It therefore becomes necessary to explain briefly the manner in which such terms are employed in this book. As to the term *race*, it really seems impossible to frame a satisfactory definition. It is best to confine its use as far as possible to the main divisions of mankind which have important physical characters in common. Thus all woolly-haired peoples (Ulotrichi) may be said to belong to one race; but usually the Negrilloes, Bushmen, Negroes, Papuans, and others, are spoken of as races. The Jews, although not of absolutely pure origin, are generally, but from this point of view erroneously, spoken of as a race; again there is no such thing as an English or an Irish race.

A *people* is a community inhabiting any given area independent of race. For example, the Andaman Islanders are a people of pure race, while the people of Ceylon belong to various races. In some cases, where racial mixture is suspected, it is better to employ this term rather than "race"; thus it is preferable to speak of the Melanesian peoples rather than of the Melanesian race.

A *tribe* may be defined as a group of a simple kind occupying a circumscribed area, having a common language, common government, and a common action in warfare.

A *nation* is a complex group which may consist of various tribes or groups, speaking different languages, but united under a common government for external affairs. The constituents of a nation usually, however, speak the same language.

A CLASSIFICATION OF MANKIND

IF we accept the character of the hair as a basis of classification, we may divide mankind into the following groups:—

ULOTRICHI:

Pygmies:

Negritoes (Andamanese, Semang of the Malay Peninsula and Sumatra, Pygmies of the Philippines), and Negrilloes of the equatorial forests of Africa.

Short and yellow-skinned:

Bushmen of South Africa.

Hottentots of South Africa.

Short or tall, and dark-skinned:

Negroes and Bantu of Africa.

Papuans and Melanesians of the West Pacific.

CYMOTRICHI are divisible into several main divisions according to their skin-colour; the great majority are dolichocephalic.

Dolichocephalic:

Melanous, or dark group:

Pre-Dravidians: Veddas of Ceylon; Kadirs, Kurumbas, Irulas, and other Jungle Tribes of the Deccan; Sakai of the Malay Peninsula and Sumatra; Toalas of Celebes; Australians.

Dravidians of the Deccan.

Ethiopians or Hamites of North-East Africa.

B

Intermediate shades:
    Indo-Afghans.
    Indonesians.
    Polynesians.
Tawny white:
    Semites.
    Mediterraneans of South Europe and North
        Africa.
Fair:
    Nordics of North Europe.
Mesaticephalic:
    Ainu of Japan.
Brachycephalic:
    Alpines (with Anatolian and Cevenole
        varieties).

LEIOTRICHI.   The straight-haired groups of mankind
are mainly confined to Asia and America.

Brachycephalic:
    Ural-Altaians: Palæasiatics, Tungus, Ko-
    reans, Mongols, together with the modified
    Ugrians and Turki; Indo-Chinese: Tibetans,
    Himalayans, Chinese, most of the natives
    of further India and Indo-China, including
    the Proto-Malays.
Dolichocephalic American Indians:
    Eskimo.
    Palæo-Amerinds.
Mesaticephalic or Brachycephalic American
    Indians :
    Patagonians, Southern Amerinds, Central
    Amerinds, North Western Amerinds,
    Northern Amerinds.

A linear arrangement, such as is practically unavoidable
in a book, can very rarely indicate biological affinities; to
illustrate these a two- or three-dimensional arrangement
is necessary.   Therefore, a tabulation, such as the above,

must not be regarded as representing all the relations between certain groups.

The **Ulotrichi** are divisible as follows:—

The Pygmy Ulotrichi are:—

Andamanese : Frizzly black hair with a reddish tinge; very dark skin; stature about 1·485m. (4ft. 10½in.),* with well-proportioned body and small hands; head small and brachycephalic (index 82)*; face broad at cheekbones; lips full but not everted; chin small but not retreating; nose much sunken at the root but straight and small; eyes prominent. Andaman Islands.

Semang : These are closely allied to the Andamanese. They have crisp woolly, brownish black hair; dark chocolate brown skin, approximating to black; stature of 1·49m. (4ft. 10¾in.) and are sturdily built; head mesaticephalic (index 78·9); round face; full lips; short flattened nose; widely open eyes. Malay Peninsula and East Sumatra.

Negritoes of the Philippines, or *Aetas :* Woolly black hair, sometimes tinged with red. The men often have abundant growth on face, chest, and limbs; skin of a dark sooty-brown colour; stature 1·474m. (4ft. 10in.); the body being slender and the arms long; the head is large in proportion and mesaticephalic (index 80); forehead broad and rounded; jaw and teeth projecting; lips thick and the under one everted; nose broad at nostrils and sunken at root; eyes deep-set and wide apart.·

Negrilloes : Hair very short and woolly, usually of a dark rusty brown colour, sometimes very dark; face hair

---

* The figures of the stature and cephalic index given in this table are averages of males. There is a considerable range in most cases, but the data here presented will serve to give a fairly correct idea of the racial types.

variable, but the body usually covered with a light, downy hair; skin reddish or yellowish brown, sometimes very dark; stature from 1·378m. to 1·452m. (4ft. 4¼in. to 4ft. 9¼in.); sometimes steatopygic;* head mesaticephalic (index 79); sometimes prognathic; lips usually thin, and the upper one long; nose broad and exceptionally long; eyes protuberant. Equatorial forests of Africa.

The short, yellow-skinned Ulotrichi are:—

Bushmen: Short, black, woolly hair, which becomes rolled up into little knots; skin yellow; stature 1·529m. (5ft. ¼in.); steatopygia is especially marked in women; hands and feet very small; very small skull, markedly low in crown, dolichocephalic (index 76); straight face with prominent cheekbones and bulging forehead; nose extremely broad, the Bushmen being the most platyrrhine of all mankind; no lobe to the ear. Now mainly confined to the Kalahari desert.

Hottentots: A cross between Bushmen and Hamites or Bantus, in which the characters of the first predominate; mongrel peoples have also arisen, mainly from Boer-Hottentot parentage. Short, woolly, black hair, with tendency to become rolled up into little knots; skin brownish yellow, sometimes tinged with grey or red; stature 1·604m. (5ft. 3in.); tendency to steatopygia; head small and dolichocephalic (index 74); face prognathic, with small chin and prominent cheekbones. South-west Africa.

---

*Steatopygia is the name given to a large development of fatty tissue in the buttocks; it is characteristic of some of the more primitive races of Africa, more especially among the Bushmen, but it must not be confounded with the general development of fat which occurs among other African peoples. Steatopygia also occurred among some of the prehistoric cave-dwellers of France.

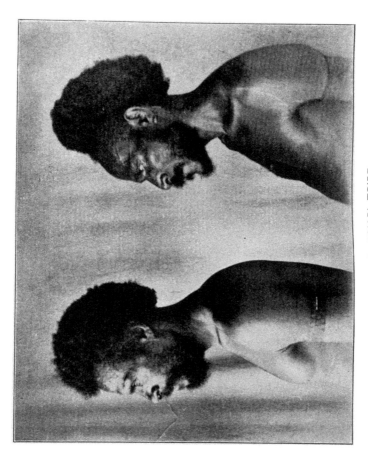

PAPUANS, KOIARI TRIBE.

[Races of Man. p. 11

Plate II.

The short or tall, dark-skinned Ulotrichi are :—
Negroes. The true Negroes are divisible into two main
stocks.—

> *Western Sudanese or Nigritian :* Hair frizzly; dark
> brown or black skin; stature 1·73 m. (5ft. 8in.);
> burly, short-legged and long-armed; dolichoce-
> phalic (index 74-75); frequently prognathous;
> forehead often bulging; thick, and often everted
> lips; platyrrhine. Guinea Coast and, originally,
> tropical Africa.

> *Eastern Sudanese or Nilotic Negroes :* Very dark skin,
> sometimes with reddish tinge; tall and slim,
> with long legs; narrow, elongated head; retreat-
> ing forehead; everted lips. Sudan and upper
> Nile valley.

Bantu : The numerous peoples of Central and Southern
Africa who speak Bantu languages present a great
variety of types. They are a Negro people mixed
with Hamitic and other elements. Hair uniformly
of the ordinary Negro type; stature 1·64-1·715 m.
(5ft 4½-7½in.); dolichocephalic—there is a brachycephalic element with lower stature, 1·594 m. (5ft. 2in.);
fatty deposits are of frequent occurence, more frequently among the women; usually skin less dark,
stature lower, head less elongated, prognathism less
marked, forehead flatter, nose generally more prominent and narrower than in the true Negroes. Africa,
south of 4 deg. N. Lat., but including the Cameroons
and excluding the Great Rift Valley plateau and the
extreme south-west of Africa.

Papuans : Black, woolly hair, often of considerable
length; dark chocolate skin; usually of medium
stature, but variable; dolichocephalic (index 73);
prognathous; platyrrhine, nose sometimes aquiline.
New Guinea, and originally throughout Melanesia,
Australia and Tasmania.

Melanesians : More variable than Papuans, and have
sometimes curly, and even wavy hair (doubtless due
to racial mixture) ; skin often lighter than Papuans,
being chocolate or occasionally copper coloured;
stature of men ranges from 1·50-1·78 m. (4ft. 11in. to
5ft. 10in.), the predominating heights are from 1·56 m.
(5ft. 1½in.) to 1·6 m. (5ft. 3in.) ; cephalic index 67-85,
but dolichocephaly prevails generally, though brachycephaly may locally predominate; nose platyrrhine,
sometimes aquiline, sometimes straight or flattened.
Bismarck Archipelago to New Caledonia, Fiji, some
parts of New Guinea.

The **Cymotrichi** are divisible into several main
groups, according to their skin colour; the great majority
are dolichocephalic.

Dolichocephalic Cymotrichi, with dark brown to nearly
black skin are :—

Veddas : These aboriginals of Ceylon are perhaps the
most primitive survivals of a Pre-Dravidian race.
Their hair is long, black, coarse, wavy or curly; skin
dark brown; stature 1·533m. (5ft. ½in.); smallest
human skull, extremely dolichocephalic (index 70·5);
orthognathic, broad face, with thin lips and pointed
chin; forehead slightly retreating, with brow arches
pointed; nose depressed at root, almost platyrrhine.

Jungle Tribes of the Deccan : There are various jungle
tribes in the Deccan, such as the Kadirs, Kurumbas,
and Irulas, which are characterised by short stature,
generally about 1·601m. (5ft. 3in.) or less, dolichocephaly, and marked platyrrhiny.

Sakai : Perhaps belonging here are the Sakai, jungle
tribes of the Malay Peninsula and East Sumatra.
Hair long, wavy or curly, black with reddish tinge;
skin yellowish brown to dark brown; stature 1·504m.
(4ft. 11¼in.); mesaticephalic (index 78); orthognathous; nose mesorrhine, bordering on platyrrhine.

These appear to have mixed with other peoples, but are now regarded as mainly of Pre-Dravidian origin.

Toala : Hair very wavy and even curly; skin darkish brown; stature 1·575m. (5ft. 2in.); they have low brachycephaly (index 82); face somewhat short; thick lips; strongly platyrrhine nose. South-west peninsula of Celebes. These people seem to be undoubtedly of Pre-Dravidian origin, though some mixture has since taken place.

Australians : A fairly uniform people, probably of mainly Pre-Dravidian stock. Curly hair; skin dark chocolate brown; stature 1·67m. (5ft. 5¾in.); dolichocephalic (index 72); prognathous; platyrrhine. Some of the Australians, at any rate, appear to have mixed with a Papuan population that preceded them in Australia.

Dravidians : This is a general term for the short dark peoples of the Deccan. The hair is plentiful, with an occasional tendency to curl; stature usually 1·626m. (5ft. 4in.); dolichocephalic (index 74-76); typically mesorrhine. Some Dravidians exhibit traces of a Pre-Dravidian strain.

Ethiopians or *Hamites* of North-East Africa include the Ancient and Modern Egyptians (in part), Beja, Galla, Somali, Abyssinians (with Arab mixture); mixed with Negroes are the Zandeh (Niam Niam), Fulah, Masai, etc. Perhaps this is a very ancient admixture of Semite with Negro. Hair usually frizzly; red-brown skin; stature 1·67-1·708 m. (5ft. 5¾in.-7¼in.); mesaticephalic (index 75-78); face elongated; not prognathous; lips thin or slightly turned; nose usually prominent, leptorrhine to mesorrhine.

Dolichocephalic Cymotrichi of intermediate shades are :—

Indo-Afghans : Dark brunets with a complexion of a very light transparent brown; stature moderate,

culminating in certain Rajputs to 1·748 m. (5ft.8¾in.);
dolichocephalic; face long; features regular; nose
straight or convex, narrow and finely cut.

Indonesians: Throughout the East Indian Archipelago
and extending into further India is a race with undulating black hair, often tinged with red; tawny skin,
often rather light; low stature of 1·54-1.57 m. (5ft.
½-1¾in.); mesaticephalic head (index 76-78), probably
originally dolichocephalic; cheekbones sometimes
projecting; nose often flattened, sometimes concave.
It is difficult to isolate this Indonesian type as it has
almost everywhere been mixed with a brachycephalic
Proto-Malay stock, but the Muruts of Borneo (cranial
index 73) are probably typical.

Polynesians: These may be regarded as a mixed variety
of the Indonesian race which has greatly increased
in stature, 1·72 m. (5ft. 7¾in.); dolichocephaly and
mesaticephaly are widely spread in Polynesia, but
there are brachycephalic centres in Tonga, the
Marquesas and the Hawaiian Islands; the broaden-
ing of the head is probably due to an early mixture
with a Proto-Malay stock; nose prominent, sometimes convex. This variety extends from Hawaii to
New Zealand, and from Samoa to Easter Island.

Of tawny white complexion are:—

Semites : Jet-black hair; stature 1·625-1·65 m. (5ft. 4-5in.)
dolichocephalic (index 70); elongated face, fine
regular features; straight or aquiline nose; the most
pure type, with a narrow straight nose, is met with
among the Arabs of South Arabia. The Jews are a
mixed people who may have acquired their so-called
"Jewish nose" from the Assyrioids or Hittites; the
latter are now probably represented by the Armenians. Their original home was in South-Western
Asia, more especially in Arabia; but they have
wandered afar, mainly into North Africa.

ARAB.

Plate III.]   [*Races of Man, p.* 14

AINU.

Plate IV.]

Mediterraneans: Hair brown or black, with fair representatives about the Atlas Mountains; stature about
1·63 m. (5ft. 4¼in.); dolichocephalic (index 72-76);
face oval; nose leptorrhine or mesorrhine; eyes
generally very dark. The Ancient Egyptians (in
part), the Libyans, Iberians, Ligurians and Pelasgians,
and the dolichocephalic (cranial index 73-74), neolithic inhabitants of Western Europe and the British
Islands belonged to this stock. Their present
distribution is mainly round the shores of the
Mediterranean.

The fairest of all peoples are :—

Nordics or "*Teutonic* Race": Yellow, very light brown,
or reddish hair, and blue or grey eyes; reddish-white
complexion; tall, with stature of 1·73m. (5ft. 8in.);
mesaticephalic (index 76-79 in the living); long face;
narrow aquiline nose. Their original home was
North Europe.

Mesaticephalic Cymotrichi:

Ainu: The indigenous population of Japan consisted of
the Ainu, who are characterised by a great profusion
of black wavy hair; short, thick-set; mesaticephalic
(index 77·8); orthognathous, with broad face; short,
fairly broad nose; large horizontal eyes, Mongolian
fold usually absent. Bälz regards them as more or
less related to the Alpine or "Celto-Slavic" Race,
but Deniker classes them as Palæasiatics, and Keane
places them, along with Semites and Dravidians, in
the Homo Mediterranensis group of the "Caucasic
Peoples."

The Brachycephalic Cymotrichi may be conveniently
included under the term *Alpines* or "*Alpine Race.*"
This race consists of a short and a tall variety. The
race occurs mainly in the plateaus and mountains that
extend from the Himalayas, through Asia Minor, the
Balkan Peninsula to Central France and Brittany.

Cevenole: This name may be applied to the short, thick-set variety which mainly occurs in Europe. Light chestnut or dark hair; hazel grey eyes; dull white skin; stature 1·63-1·64m. (5ft. 4-4½in.); cephalic index 85-87; broad face; rather broad heavy nose.

Dinaric or *Adriatic*: A tall variety, stature 1·68-1·72m. (5ft. 6-7¾in.), which is probably an offshoot from the Anatolian.

Anatolian or *Armenian*: The former name may be given to the tall variety of Asia Minor. The Armenians appear to be the modified representatives of an ancient Hittite stock. They are characterised by a tawny white skin; stature 1·63-1·69m. (5ft. 4¼-6½in.); the body is heavy, with a tendency to corpulency; brachycephalic head, which is very flat behind (index 85-87); aquiline nose with a depressed tip and large wings is very characteristic.

Leiotrichi: The straight-haired groups of mankind, who are also mainly brachycephalic, are chiefly confined to Asia and America.

Palæasiatics or *Eastern Siberians*: The head is often mesaticephalic; but in most of their features, flat face, prominent cheek bones, oblique eyes, yellowish brown colour, low stature, long, lank hair and sparse beard, they resemble other Siberian groups. They inhabit the north-east corner of Asia, and include the Yukaghirs, Koryaks, Chukchis, Kamchadales and Gilyaks; the latter appear to have mixed with the Ainu, which would account for the more regular features and beards of some of them.

Tungus: The Tungus group is subject to considerable variation. The northern members resemble in the main the Palæasiatics—for example, the Tungus, Orochons, Lamuts and Gold. The Manchus are taller, slighter, and with a tendency towards mesaticephaly.

Koreans: The modification of the Tungus type exhibited in the Manchus is intensified in the Koreans, who are tall and slender, with a cephalic index of 82; long, narrow, and frequently prognathous face; narrow aquiline nose; eyes with Mongolian fold; long, thin beard.

Mongols: The skin varies in colour from pale yellowish to yellowish brown; black straight hair, little hair on face or body; stature 1·635m. (5ft. 3¾in.); brachycephalic (index 82-84) with a low vault; cheekbones prominent; flattened face, Mongolian eyes. Typical Mongols are the Sharras, of whom the Khalkas, who inhabit the whole Gobi area, are the most important group. The Kalmuks live to the west of the Khalka country, mainly in Zungaria and the northern part of Kashgaria; an outlier also occurs north-west of the Caspian. The Buryats to the north are somewhat mixed, and extend east and west of the southern half of Lake Baikal.

Turki: Yellowish white complexion, some with much hair on the face, medium stature 1·675 m. (5ft. 6in.), with a tendency to obesity; a brachycephalic high head (index 85-87); elongated oval face; straight, somewhat prominent nose; eyes not Mongolian. The eastern group comprises the Yakuts of the Lena basin and certain so-called Tatars; the central group contains the Kirghiz, Kazaks, Uzbegs, etc. of Russian Turkistan; the western is composed mainly of the Turkomans, east of the Caspian, and of the Osmanli in Asia Minor and Turkey. To this group belonged the Ughuz and the dreaded Uighurs, who once founded a civilised state in Northern Kashgaria (Chinese Turkistan).

Ugrians: Generally speaking, the Ugrians have a yellowish white skin; the hair may be black or brown; they are generally of short stature; mesaticephalic or brachycephalic; projecting cheek bones; straight or concave nose. Keane employs the terms Ugrian Finns or Ugro-Finns; and Deniker calls the Asiatic tribes, Yeniseians or Tubas. The peoples of Western Siberia mainly belong to this group, such as the Ostyaks, Tuba, Voguls, Samoyads; the Votyaks and Cheremiss have penetrated into Russia, and the Lapps into Northern Scandinavia. The latter have a stature of 1·53 m. (5ft. ¼in.), a cephalic index of 87, with a correspondingly broad face, prominent cheek bones, dark brown hair, and a yellowish white skin; like most Ugrians they have an ungainly figure. Great modifications have taken place in some of the peoples, who, belonging to this stock, have migrated into Europe, such as the Finns, Esthonians, Livonians, Bulgars, Magyars, and others.

Indo-Chinese, Pareœans or *Southern Mongols*: Hair black and lank, little hair on the face; skin colour varies from yellowish in the north to olive and coppery-brown in the south; stature varies a good deal, but is generally short, averaging about 1·6 m. (5ft. 3in.); often thick set; brachycephalic (index 80-85); frequently prognathic; nose short and broad; eyes often very oblique, with Mongolian fold. Most of the peoples of this group are considerably mixed with other races; they comprise the Tibetans, Himalayans, Chinese proper, and the bulk of the populations of further India and Indo-China. Those members who spread into the East Indian Archipelago are often called Oceanic Mongols, but a better term is Proto-Malays; and it is from these the true Malay is derived.

Dolichocephalic American Indians:—

Eskimo: The pure Eskimo are a very distinct group, with a brownish or reddish-yellow complexion; stature of 1·575 m. (5ft. 2in.); they are dolichoce-

Plate V.]

CHINESE.

phalic (index 71-72), with a high vault; they have a broad face, projecting cheek bones; and eyes straight and black.

Palæo-Amerinds: Deniker recognises a short dolichocephalic South American Palæo-American type with wavy or even curly hair which is still recognisable in the mesaticephals. The cranial index of the Botocudos is 73·9.

Mesaticephalic or Brachycephalic American Indians:—

Patagonians: The brachycephalic Patagonians (index 85) are of a brown colour; tall stature averaging 1·73-1·83 m. (5ft. 8in.-6ft.); and square face. Traces of this stock are found in Central South America.

Southern Amerinds: Mesaticephalic or brachycephalic; with yellow skin, smooth body; straight or concave nose; and short stature.

Central Amerinds: Brachycephalic, with brownish-yellow or brown skin; low stature; and straight or aquiline nose.

North-Western Amerinds of the Pacific slope: Brachycephalic (index of 82-85); they have usually a rounded face; and stature of 1·66-1·69 m. (5ft 5¼in.-6½in.).

Northern Amerinds of the Atlantic slope: Mesaticephalic; with warm yellow skin; oval face; straight or aquiline nose; and stature of 1·68-1·75 m. (5ft. 6-9in.).

DISTRIBUTION OF RACES AND PEOPLES
ACCORDING TO AREAS

OCEANIA

OCEANIA comprises Australia, Melanesia, Polynesia and Micronesia.

It is generally believed that Australia was originally inhabited, or at all events in parts, by Papuans or Negritoes, or more probably by a stock intermediate between them, who wandered on foot to the extreme south of that continent. When Bass' Strait was formed, those who were cut off from the mainland formed the ancestors of the Tasmanians, who never advanced beyond an early stage of stone-age culture. Later, a Pre-Dravidian race migrated into Australia, and over-ran the continent and absorbed the sparse aboriginal population. Since then they have practically remained isolated from the rest of the world. Their languages bear no relation to the Austronesian or Oceanic linguistic family.

Melanesia includes New Guinea and the neighbouring islands, and the chain of archipelagoes that extends from the Admiralties to New Caledonia, including Fiji. For the sake of clearness these will be termed the Melanesian Archipelago. The inhabitants of this area are sometimes spoken of as Oceanic Negroes. The primitive stock appears to have been a very dark coloured and invariably woolly-haired people, to whom the name Papuans can perhaps be best applied. They form the majority of the inhabitants of New Guinea and the basis of the populations of the Melanesian Archipelago. The latter peoples speak a language which is a primitive form of the Austric linguistic family, whereas the Papuan languages belong to a different family.   Certain physical traits and cultural developments also indicate that foreign influences have modified the original stock.   The view now commonly held is that the Melanesian Archipelago was originally inhabited by Papuans, and perhaps also by Negritoes, and that the Proto-Polynesians in their migration from the East Indian Archipelago to Polynesia passed through this region and imposed their speech on the population and otherwise modified it.   In later times parts of Melanesia have been directly influenced by movements from Polynesia.   The result of these supposed influences has been to form the Melanesian peoples as they exist to-day. Settlements from the Melanesian Archipelago occur along the greater part of the coast of South-east New Guinea.

The Polynesians are a mixed people.   Their original home was perhaps somewhere in Eastern India, whence, shortly before our era, they migrated to the East Indian Archipelago, where we may speak of them as Indonesians. The Proto-Malays were about this time pressing down south from the mainland of Asia, and eventually a mixed population seems to have gone further east.   Probably the Proto-Polynesians, as they may now be termed, settled for some time in the northern portion of the Melanesian Archipelago, where some mixture took place. Perhaps about 450 A.D. they began to adventure into the Pacific.   Samoa was certainly colonised in 600 A.D., and Hawaii first settled in 650 A.D.   Voyages from the south to Hawaii ceased in 1325 A.D.   New Zealand was visited in 850 A.D., but "the fleet" did not arrive till 1350 A.D.   The darker skinned and more curly haired peoples who occur in some of the eastern Polynesian islands may be the remains of a half-breed class of low rank due to the sojourn in Melanesia.   The bulk of the Polynesians, however, show very little trace of this mixture.

The Micronesians have much the same origin as the Polynesians, but many exhibit more direct traces of Asiatic influence.

Australians.

The Australians can rarely depend on regular supplies of food. They feed on flesh, fish, grubs, insects and wild vegetable food. Cultivation of the soil is unknown, except that on the west coast the natives invariably re-insert the head of the wild yams they have dug up so as to be sure of a future crop. The cultivation of purslane seems to be a well-established fact. The Australians are expert hunters and trackers, and make use of ingenious devices for catching fish and land animals. The game caught by a man has to be shared with others according to rule. There are many food taboos. Cannibalism is widely spread, but human flesh is nowhere a regular article of food. There are no domesticable animals except the introduced dingo. Clothing of every description, apart from ornament, is rarely worn; but in the south skin cloaks are commonly used, and occasionally fur aprons. Scarification of the body is very frequent, and prominent cicatrices are often made. Dwellings are usually of the simplest character, being breakwinds or slight huts; but in places permanent huts are constructed of boughs covered with bark and grass, and sometimes coated with clay. Implements are made of shell, bone, wood and stone. Spears and wooden clubs are universal; many of the spears are thrown by hand, but very generally some are projected by means of a spear-thrower. The use of the boomerang is nearly universal; the variety that returns when it is thrown is in most tribes only a plaything; it is, however, used for throwing at birds. There are no bows and arrows. Pottery is unknown. Rafts are made of one or more logs, and the commonest form of canoe is that made of a single sheet of bark.

The Australians are divided into tribes of varying size,

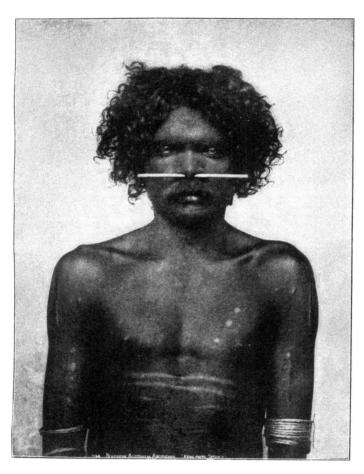

NORTHERN AUSTRALIAN.

Plate VI.]

who occupy a certain tract of hunting ground in common, speak dialects of the same language, and acknowledge a common relatedness to each other which they deny to all other tribes. Tribes are divided into well-defined local groups, each having rights over a definite portion of the common country, and these are sub-divided until the smallest unit consists of a few people of the same blood under the leadership of one of the ablest elder men. The grouping of individuals under the names of plants, animals, or various objects is practically universal; these are termed totem septs, clans, or kins. The members commonly believe themselves to be actually descended from, or related to, their totem, and all members are regarded as brethren, though they may belong to different local communities or tribes. The totem is rarely injured, killed or eaten, and members of the totem sept must help and never injure each other. Typically each totem sept is exogamous. Usually the totem septs of a tribe are grouped into two exogamous moieties, frequently termed phratries, each of which may be divided into two or four exogamous classes. Descent in the classes is indirect matrilineal or indirect patrilineal, that is, while the child still belongs to the mother's or the father's moiety (as the case may be) it is assigned to the class of that society to which the mother or the father does not belong; but the grandchildren belong to the class of the grandmother or grandfather. Thus descent in an indirect matrilineal group is as follows:—

Moiety.	Man of class	marries	Woman of class.	Their children are members of class
A	a	=	b	b
	a	=	b	b
B	b	=	a	a
	b	=	a	a

The classificatory system of relationship terms prevails. Descent is reckoned through the mother in some tribes and through the father in others. The local group has perpetual succession through males.

Among many tribes there are two kinds of marital relation, but in every case the marriage can only take place between the members of certain groups. Thus in most tribes all the women are either actual or potential wives, or sisters of the men of their own tribe. A person of marriageable age may be allocated to a special spouse, and to a varying number of accessory spouses for varying periods. In other tribes individual marriage occurs with an increasing limitation of the rights of other members of the community.

Each totem and local group has its head man, within which area alone he exercises power The head men constitute the council of the tribe, and generally one is chief.

Beneficent and malevolent magic are universally practised. Besides its social side totemism has its religious aspect. An emotional relation often exists between the members of the totem sept and the totem, and in some cases the totem warns or protects its human kinsmen. Certain tribes perform elaborate ceremonies, which are designed to render the totem prolific, or to insure its abundance. Most tribes believe in mythical beings, and a belief in a vague supreme being or elder in the sky appears to be widely spread

Papuans and Melanesians.

The Melanesians are a noisy, excitable, demonstrative, affectionate, cheery, passionate people. They could not be hunters everywhere, as in most islands there is no game, nor could they be pastors anywhere, as there are no cattle; the only resources are fishing and agriculture. In New Guinea and the West Solomons the sago palm is of great importance. Coco-nut palms grow mainly on the shore in most islands. The main crops are various kinds of bananas, numerous kinds of yams, bread-fruit, taro (caladium) and sweet potatoes.

The men go nude in some of the wilder parts, but mostly they wear a perineal band, which may be broad or merely a string. Almost everywhere the women wear a longer or shorter petticoat of finely shredded leaves. The darker coloured natives decorate their skin by cicatrices and cheloids. True tattooing is employed sporadically. Every portion of the body is decorated in various ways with shells, teeth, feathers, leaves, flowers, and other objects, and bands are plaited to ornament the neck, trunk, and limbs. Especially characteristic of Melanesia are shell necklaces, which constitute a kind of currency, and artificially deformed boars' tusks.

The typical Melanesian house has a roof of bamboo bent over a ridge pole which is supported by two main posts, very low side walls, and the ends filled in with bamboo screens. Pile dwellings are found in New Britain, some of the Solomons, and in New Guinea, where they are sometimes in the sea.

Bows and arrows occur in New Guinea, except in the south-east end, and generally in the archipelago. Spears are used in the greater part of New Guinea and the northern archipelago. Stone-headed clubs are found in New Guinea and New Hebrides, wooden clubs are universal. Slings are generally distributed in the archipelago and in parts of New Guinea. Rafts and light canoes occur in the Solomons, but the hollow tree trunk with plank gunwhale is general in Melanesia.

Food is cooked in the earth-oven everywhere; stone-boiling is very widely known, boiling in clay pots is local, and sometimes large shells are employed for boiling. Wooden vessels for preparing and cooking food are commonly distributed. Pottery is made at a few places in New Guinea, and sporadically in the archipelago.

A division of the community into two exogamous groups is very widely spread, no intermarriage being permitted within the group. Mother-right is very prevalent, descent and inheritance being counted on the mother's side, and a man's property descends to his sister's children; but the mother is in no way the head of the family; the house is the father's, the garden may be his, the rule and government are his, though the maternal uncle sometimes has more authority than the father. The transition to father-right has definitely occurred in various places, and is taking place elsewhere; thus, in some of the New Hebrides the father has to buy off the rights of his wife's relations or his sister's children. The classificatory system of relationship-terms very generally prevails. Totemism has marked socialising effects, as totemic solidarity takes precedence of all other considerations. It occurs in some parts of Southern New Guinea, Fiji, and other islands in the archipelago, where it is becoming obsolete. Almost everywhere in a village there is one building (often two, sometimes more) of a public character where men eat and spend their time, in these young men sleep, and strangers are entertained; in the Solomons these are also canoe-houses. Frequently they contain images; women are excluded from them. In the Banks Islands and New Hebrides there are numerous clubs, the members of which are of many strictly marked grades, promotion being by payment; each rank has its insignia, sometimes human effigies, which are usually but wrongly spoken of as "idols." Other socialising factors are feasts, dances, markets, and money.

Probably everywhere public affairs are regulated by discussion among the old or important men; the more primitive the society the more important this is. Chiefs exist everywhere, though with variable powers, which mainly depend upon their own character, but in many places their influence is attributed to their *mana*. Hereditary chieftainship in the direct line rarely occurs, though it is often retained in the family. Every village has its own chief who alone rules, but weaker chiefs join in offensive and defensive alliances, and powerful chiefs sometimes force weaker ones into vassalship. The power of secret societies tends to obscure that of the chiefs. Practically no organisation exists for redressing wrong or punishing the guilty, hence private quarrels are personal affairs and public opinion stops them only when they become acute. The growth of the power of secret societies forms a means for the coercion and chastisement of objectionable persons, but they are often terrorising and black-mailing institutions. They occur in New Guinea (except the south-east peninsula) and New Britain, and from Torres Islands to New Caledonia, and with them are frequently associated awesome ceremonies with masked performers and implements that produce weird sounds.

Important secret initiation ceremonies for lads take place in the bush or in special houses in various parts of New Guinea, New Britain, some of the Solomons, and Malekula. Magical practices occur everywhere for the gaining of benefits, plenteous crops, good fishing, fine weather, rain, success in love, and the procuring of children. Harmful magic for producing sickness and death is universal.

From the Solomons to the New Hebrides (and perhaps elsewhere) the native mind is entirely possessed by belief in a supernatural power or influence, called almost universally *mana*. This is what works to effect everything which is beyond the ordinary power of man or outside the common processes of nature; but this power, though in itself impersonal, is always connected with some person who directs it; all spirits have it, ghosts generally, and some men (Codrington). Animism does not exist; the sea or forest does not possess its own soul, but is haunted by spirit or ghost; Animatism, or intrinsic life in inanimate objects, does occur in some places. A more or less developed ancestor cult is universally distributed. Human beings may become beneficent or maleficent ghosts, but not every ghost becomes an object of regard. The ghost who is to be worshipped is the spirit of a man who in his lifetime had *mana*. Hero cult occurs in Torres Straits. Good or evil spirits apparently independent of ancestors are found practically everywhere. In the Solomons more attention is paid to ghosts with a greater development of sacrifice, offerings of food being burnt as well as eaten (associated with these is an advance in the arts of life). In the southern groups more attention is paid to the spirits; food, and more especially money, is offered to them, but not burnt or eaten, and generally offered at stones sacred to spirits. There are no priests, but a man who knows how to perform magic or approach an object of worship sometimes sacrifices for all. There are no " idols." Everywhere life after death is believed in.

Polynesians.

The Polynesians are cheerful, dignified and polite, and more imaginative and intelligent but more dissolute than the Melanesians. They are very cleanly in their habits and neat and orderly.

Wherever possible they are agriculturists, growing yams, sweet potatoes, and taro. Coco-nut, bread-fruit, and bananas form the staple food in many islands. Cannibalism was prevalent in Polynesia; it was resorted to sometimes for purposes of revenge, sometimes it had a magical significance. Human flesh appears to have been eaten simply for food in New Zealand and other places.

MAORI.

Plate VII.]   Races of Man, p. 28.

The men formerly wore an adequate garment of bark cloth (tapa), and the women an ample petticoat made of native cloth or of leaves split and coarsely plaited. Ornaments are more sparingly worn than in Melanesia, with the exception of flowers. The houses are well built, usually with thatched walls and roof, and are oval or oblong in form. The bow and arrow is unknown as a weapon; short spears, slings, and wooden clubs are used, but no shields. Fishing is everywhere resorted to, and fish-hooks are made in great variety. Pottery was made only in the Tonga and Easter Islands. Mat-making and basketry are carried to a fine art, as is the making of tapa. The old feather work attained its greatest excellence in Hawaii. Large sailing double canoes were formerly in use, and single canoes with an outrigger are still made.

All through Polynesia the community is divided into nobles or chiefs, freemen and slaves, which divisions are by reason of taboo as sharp as those of caste. They fall into those which participate in the divine and those which are wholly excluded from it. Women have a high position, and men do their fair share of work. Polygyny was universal, being limited only by the wealth of the husband or the numerical preponderance of the men. The husband can take nothing of his wife's; when he dies she retains only what he has given her, his brother being the heir. Mother-right was universal, but father-right has begun in places, especially in the families of chiefs. Children inherit their mother's rank and property.

Usually the priests gained considerable influence, and there were numerous gods. In Samoa and Tonga the primitive gods were associated with animals, and sometimes entered their bodies. Excluding Samoa, gods were worshipped by " idols " which were not " gods " but " god-boxes "; ancestors were also deified. The system of taboo was carried to a great excess in many islands. Taboo is a Polynesian word and is said to mean strongly marked. Things holy and things unclean are alike taboo. Tabooed persons render everything they touch taboo; its operation is always mechanical, and the intentions of the taboo-breaker have no effect upon the action of the taboo.

AFRICA.

AFRICA proper begins south of Sahara. The northern desert zone and the Mediterranean area are the home of the horse. The camel is the typical domestic animal of the desert zone. At the base of the northern slopes of the plateau spiny shrubs give pasturage for goats. Further south the greater rainfall gives rise to a vigorous flora, and cows graze on the luxuriant grass; here, too, the natives grow durra (sorghum); Eleusine is grown in the drier region north of the Welle. The increased rainfall of West and Central Africa permits the growth of dense forests; the banana is the chief food plant, and in Uganda it is the staple food. The imported manioc (cassava or tapioca) is grown in West Central Africa and south of the Congo and north of the Zambezi. Where there is sufficient moisture on the plateaus of South Africa, scattered trees constitute a savanna (bush-veld), elsewhere there is only grass (grass or high veld) except to the west, where steppes culminate in the Kalahari Desert, and it is into this inhospitable country that the Bushman has mainly retreated.

There is some evidence that at a very early time the Bushmen occupied the hunting grounds of tropical East Africa, perhaps even to the confines of Abyssinia. They gradually passed southwards, keeping along the more open grass lands of the eastern mountainous zone, where they could still preserve their hunting method of life, until, when history dawned on the scene, they roamed over most of the territory south of the Zambezi.

Culturally, as well as physically, the Hottentots may be regarded as a blend of two stocks. They combined

the cattle-rearing habits of the Hamites with the
aversion from tillage of the soil characteristic of the
hunter; they became nomadic herders, who were
stronger than the Bushmen, but who themselves could
not withstand the Bantu when they came in contact
with them, and they too were driven to less favourable
lands.

The Hottentot migration from the eastern mountainous
zone took place much later than that of the Bushmen,
and it seems to have been due mainly to the pressure
from behind of the waxing Bantu peoples.   These
pastoral nomads took a south-westerly course across the
savanna country south of lake Tanganyika, and worked
their way down the west coast and along the southern
shore of the continent.   What is now Cape Colony was
inhabited solely by Bushmen and Hottentots at the time
of the arrival of the Europeans.   As the latter expanded
they drove the aborigines before them, but in the
meantime mongrel peoples had arisen, mainly of Boer-
Hottentot parentage, who also were forced to migrate.
Those of the Cape Hottentots, who were not exterminated or enslaved, drifted north and found in
Bushmanland an asylum from their pursuers.

The Negrilloes, who primitively were probably related
to the Bushmen, appear always to have occupied the
tropical forests of Africa.   Their local variability indicates
a Negro mixture.

The home of the Negro appears to have been the
Sudan and most of the tropical area, where he practised
agriculture and became a great trader.   That branch of
the true Negro stock which spake the mother-tongue of
the Bantu languages some 3,000 years ago (according to
Sir Harry Johnston's estimate) spread over the area of
what is now Uganda and British East Africa.   In the
forest region these people probably mixed with Negrilloes,
and possibly with the most northerly representatives of

the Bushmen in the high lands to the east.   Here also they came into contact with the Hamitic peoples coming down from the north, and their amalgamation constituted a new breed of Negro—the Bantu.

The Bantu are cattle-rearers who practise agriculture. A factor of great importance in their evolution is to be found in the great diversity of climate and soil in Equatorial East Africa.   It is a country of small plateaus separated by gorges, or low-lying lands.   The small plateaus are suitable for pasturage, but their extent is limited; thus they fell to the lot of the more vigorous people, while the conquered had to content themselves with low country, and were obliged to hunt or cultivate the land.   In these healthy highlands the people multiplied, and migration became necessary; the stronger and better-organised groups retained their flocks and migrated in a southerly direction, keeping to the savannas and open country, the line of least resistance being indicated by the relative social feebleness of the peoples to the south.   In the small plateaus a nomadic life is impossible for the herders, there being at most a seasonal change of pasturage.   This prevents the possession of large herds and necessitates a certain amount of tillage; further, it would seem that this mode of life tends to develop military organisation and a tribal system.

The north-east corner of Africa, from Egypt to Somaliland, is the home of the Hamites.   Essentially they are a pastoral people, and therefore prone to wander.   In Uganda, the occasionally polyandric Bahima are of Hamitic descent; they are herdsmen in Buganda, a sort of aristocracy in Unyoro, a ruling caste in Toro, and the dominant race with dynasties in Ankole.   The dreaded Masai of East Africa seem to be a hybrid between the Negro and Galla.   Another example of the predominance which a Hamitic mixture usually engenders is seen in the "rude Fullah shepherds" who overlord the settled, industrious, and commercial Negro Hausas in the Sudan.

From time immemorial Semites have poured into Africa, and the whole country north of Sahara has been largely Semitised by Arabs of the Ishmaelitic group, but the Berbers remain as distinct as they can from the Arabs. A similar process has occurred in Abyssinia, but by the Himyaritic or Sabæan group. Arab traders and slave raiders have penetrated far into Africa, and have modified the population of the eastern coasts.

The characters of the pygmies of the equatorial forests of Africa are variable, and mixture with Negroes has taken place.

Negrilloes.

They are a markedly intelligent people, innately musical, and cunning, revengeful, and suspicious in disposition; they never steal.

They are nomadic hunters and collectors, never resorting to agriculture. They have no domestic animals. Only meat is cooked. They wear no clothing of any sort. They use bows and poisoned arrows.

Their own language is not known. They live in small communities which centre round a cunning fighter or able hunter. Their dead are buried in the ground. Nothing is known of their religion.

Bushmen.

The Bushmen, Khuai or San, have been generally credited with being vindictive, passionate, and cruel, but they were as a matter of fact always friendly and hospitable to strangers till dispossessed of their hunting grounds. They were not given to fighting one another, and were an unselfish, merry, cheerful race, with an intense love of freedom.

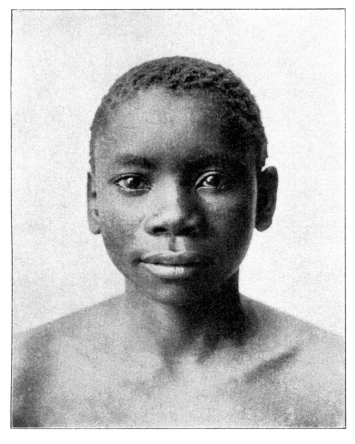

NEGRILLO, Kasai Valley, Congo.

Plate VIII.]   [*Races of Man, p.* 34.

Being nomadic hunters the Bushmen can only attain to the rudiments of material culture. Their clothing consists solely of a small skin, and there is a dearth of personal ornaments; necklaces are, however, made out of the discs of ostrich eggs. They frequently cut off the terminal joint of the little finger. Their dwellings are portable, mat-covered, dome-shaped huts, but they often live in caves, the rock walls of which they are fond of decorating with spirited coloured representations of men and animals; designs are also chipped by them on surfaces of exposed rocks. For weapons they have small bows and poisoned arrows; their only implement is a perforated rounded stone, into which a stick is inserted, and this they use for digging up roots. A little coarse pottery is occasionally made. The Bushmen were never cannibals. Cairns of stones are erected over the graves of their dead.

Hottentots.

The Hottentots, or Khoikhoi, of former days were described as mild and amiable. They were absolutely improvident, unstable, and thoughtless, and extraordinarily dirty in every respect. Sick and infirm persons and weak or deformed children were abandoned, but they never resorted to cannibalism.

They were nomadic herdsmen who never cultivated the soil. Their chief foods were milk from their herds, the flesh of such animals as died, which they ate cooked, game, locusts, and various plants and fruits. They had an intoxicating drink made of honey, and smoked a sort of wild hemp which is a powerful intoxicant.

Both sexes had clothing made of skins prepared with the hair on; that of the men consisted of a skin flap in the front and a strip at the back. Their ornaments consisted of copper trinkets, and strings of shells or leopards' teeth round the neck.

Their dwellings were portable, dome-shaped huts covered with mats, with one opening. These huts were arranged in a circle round a space used as a fold for cattle. They had wooden dishes for milk, and ostrich egg-shells were used as vessels. Their weapons were bows and poisoned arrows, assagais and knobkerries or clubbed sticks used as missiles. Clumsy earthenware pots were made for cooking.

The Hottentots were grouped in clans, each with its hereditary chief, whose authority, however, was very limited. Several clans were loosely united to form tribes. The jealousy between the head men of the clans rendered the government very unstable.

The Hottentots were polygynous, a man being allowed to have as many wives as he could afford, who were generally taken from a different clan.

The right of individuals to hold property apart from the community was recognised, and the possession of wealth entailed considerable influence. Children in herited the property of their fathers.

The Hottentots believed in charms, good and evil omens, and had a dread of ghosts and evil spirits. They sang and danced to the new moon. There was a cult of a mythical hero named Heitsi-eibib who has become magnified into the supreme power of good. There was also a powerful evil being named Gaunab, who was worsted by Heitsi-eibib.

Negroes.

In the forest regions the people subsist mainly on bananas, fish, and game, though corn, yams, earth-nuts, beans, and gourds are frequently grown. In the more open country, millet is extensively grown together with other edible plants. Hunting is everywhere indulged in. Goats, pigs, and chickens are kept almost everywhere; cattle and horses are kept only in the more open or higher regions, their distribution being largely regulated by the tsetse fly.

The clothing of the Negroes consists of bark-cloth, woven palm-fibre, and introduced cotton, and they are much addicted to vegetable ornaments. Circumcision is common, and the upper incisors are frequently knocked out. The form of dwelling is the rectangular gable-roofed hut; their weapons include spears with socketed heads, bows tapering at each end with bowstrings of vegetable products, swords, and plaited shields, but no clubs or slings. Among the musical instruments are wooden drums and a peculiar form of guitar in which each string has its own support. Head-rests and coiled basketry do not generally occur. Metal-working is met with everywhere and weaving is general; earthenware is made everywhere, and leather-working is carried to a fine art. The Negroes have always been great traders, and markets are held in all towns.

Among the more primitive tribes, the community is divided into exogamous septs which probably were originally totemic, and which trace their descent from a common ancestress. Polygyny is universal when a man can afford it, but the first wife takes precedence of the rest. Usually descent is in the female line, but occasionally it is reckoned through the father, in which case the sons inherit his property. Slavery is not so abject a condition as is often the case. Slaves may be war-captives, or a man may pawn himself or his relatives into slavery. Domestic slaves may inherit property.

Secret societies flourish in West Africa in which masks are employed. These societies are powerful engines for the regulation of society and punishment of ill-doers, although at times their power is abused. Very frequently the women also have secret societies which support their interests.

Fetishism is universal; the fetish may consist of any object whatsoever; it is accredited with mysterious power owing to its being temporarily or permanently the vessel or habitation or instrument of some unseen power or spirit. It may act by the will or force of its own power or spirit, or by force of a foreign power entering in or acting on it from without. It is worshipped, prayed to, sacrificed to, and petted or ill-treated according to its behaviour.

Animism, the belief in everything in nature being animated by an indwelling spirit of its own, is said to be prevalent. Some deities are local, but there are frequently other deities of the sky, of the earthquake, and so forth. Priests occur everywhere, but it is only among the more civilised peoples that they acquire power. A cult of ancestors is met with in all parts.

Bantus.

The Bantu peoples may be roughly divided according to culture into two groups: a western zone, which skirts the West African region or the Congo basin and extends through Angola and German West Africa into Cape Colony; and an eastern zone. (1) The western Bantu zone is characterised by beehive huts, the absence of circumcision, and the presence of wooden shields (plain or covered with cane-work) in its northern portion, though skin shields occur to the south. (2) In the eastern Bantu zone, except among the Zulu peoples, the huts are cylindrical, with a separate conical roof. Certain characteristics are typical of the Bantu culture as a whole. The natives live in rounded huts with pointed roofs. The domestic animals include the dog, goat, and sheep and cattle are found wherever possible. Clothing is of skin and leather, and there is a pre-dominance of animal ornaments; knocking out or filing of incisors is general except in the south; circumcision is common, though among the Zulu tribes it seems to be dying out. Their weapons comprise spears, in which the head is fastened into the shaft by a spike, bows with bowstrings of animal products, clubs and skin shields, but slings are usually absent. Coiled basketry is made, and head-rests are a characteristic feature.

Totemism once existed, but now only occurs in certain tribes. Ancestor-worship is the prevalent form of religion; fetishism and polytheism are undeveloped. Masks and representations of human figures are rare, and there are no secret societies, though secluded initiation ceremonies may be held. Anthropophagy is sporadic and usually temporary.

The Bantu are cattle-rearers who practise agriculture. This duality of occupation led to variability in mode of life. In some places the land invited the population towards husbandry, in others the physical conditions were more suited to a pastoral life, and thus we find settled agricultural tribes on the one hand and wandering herders on the other. The Bantu peoples easily adopt changes of custom; under the leadership of a warlike chief they become warlike and cruel, a common characteristic of pastoral peoples. The history of the prolific Bantu peoples on the whole indicates that they were as loosely attached to the soil as were the Ancient Germans, and, like the latter, at the slightest provocation, they would abandon their country and seek another home. This readiness to migrate is the direct effect of a pastoral life, and along with this legacy of unrest their Hamitic ancestors transmitted a social organisation which lent itself to discipline.

EUROPE.

THE population of Europe may be briefly described as consisting of an indigenous white population and intrusive Asiatic peoples.

In classifying the Europeans proper, the most important physical features to be noted are the cephalic index, pigmentation, and stature. The cephalic index ranges from 62 to 103, but the limit of variation in definite groups is much more restricted. Pigmentation in Europe is mainly considered with regard to the colour of hair and eyes. Dark hair and dark eyes constitute pure brunet types; fair hair and light eyes, pure blond types; their relative frequency is expressed in percentages. Pigmentation shades from 54% of pure blond types in Sweden to 96% of pure brunet types in Greece. Stature appears to be of less importance; it varies from a preponderance of heights about 1·6m. (5ft. 3in.) in Sardinia to 1·792m. (5ft. 10½in.) in Galloway (South-west Scotland).

Judged by these characters, the bulk of the existing population of true Europeans can be divided into three main groups:—(1) Tall, fair, dolichocephals in the north, (2) Short or tall, medium-coloured, brachycephals in the centre; and (3) Short, dark, dolichocephals in the south. During and since neolithic times the Nordic (Northern), Alpine, and Mediterranean "races" have existed in northern, central, and southern Europe, but various movements and mixtures of portions of these three groups have occurred which have greatly complicated European racial ethnology.

The Asiatic elements in Europe are confined to its

eastern portion; they belong to the Ugrian, Turki and Mongol divisions of the Ural-Altaians.

NORTHERN EUROPE :—

SCANDINAVIA.—There are three distinct racial elements in Scandinavia :—

1. The Lapps are *Ugrians* of Asiatic origin who lived in the north of Norway and Sweden, but formerly they extended further to the South.

2. *Northern Race*, in greatest purity over the greater part of Norway, Sweden, and Denmark.

3. Round the south of Sweden, the south and west coast of Norway, and on the opposite shores of Denmark, is a brachycephalic type (index 80-83), with darker hair and eye colour, and shorter stature, thus indicating a mixture with the *Alpine Race*.

BRITISH ISLES.—Mainly inhabited by members of the *Northern* and *Mediterranean Races*, with traces of *Alpine Race*. The cephalic index is uniformly 77-78. The *Northern* elements are more pronounced on north and east of Britain, with fair colouring and tall stature. The *Mediterranean* elements persist in Inverness, Argyle, Wales, Cornwall, an area north of London, the Fen country, and largely in Ireland, with darker colouring and shorter stature. Traces of *Alpine* elements occur in Fife, East Lothian, Aberdeen, Shetland Islands, Faröe Islands, and the north-west coast of Ireland, with a cephalic index of 79-81.

CENTRAL EUROPE :—

FRANCE. — Two axes of fertility, from Flanders to Bordeaux, and along the Rhone valley, separate four less attractive areas : the Ardennes plateau, Auvergne, Savoy, and Brittany. These areas are occupied by the *Alpine Race*, with a cephalic index of 83-87, medium colouring, and short stature, especially in Auvergne. The axes of fertility are occupied by the *Northern Race* to the north, and the *Mediterranean Race* to the south; the cephalic index ranges from 79 to 83; blondness and stature decrease from north to south.

In Dordogne a type is met with which has a cephalic index of 76 to 78, a low vault, broad face, prominent cheekbones, dark colouring, and a medium stature. This is regarded as a survival of the *Cro-Magnon* type, which dates from late Palæolithic times.

In Brittany, the fringe of *Northern Race* round the coast is due to Saxon invasions, especially noticeable in the predominance of fair types in Morbihan. There are traces of a Cornish settlement near Dinan.

The Basques are placed by Deniker in his *Littoral* or *Atlanto-Mediterranean Race*. They are brachycephalic (index 83) north of the Pyrenees; and mesaticephalic (index 77-79) south of the Pyrenees; the dividing line being over the north slope of the range. The facial features found among both types are a triangular face, broad temples, long pointed chin, long thin nose, dark hair, dark eyes rather close together, and a stature of 1·65m. to 1·674m. (5ft. 5in. to 5ft. 6in.). The Basques are generally regarded as a variety of the *Mediterranean Race.*

SWITZERLAND.—The *Alpine Race* is predominant, and the *Northern Race* subordinate; cephalic index 87; hair and eye colour medium; stature, 1·67m. (5ft. 5¾in.).

BELGIUM.—The Flemings of the northern plains belong to the *Northern Race;* cephalic index 79. The Walloons of the southern uplands are members of the *Alpine Race;* cephalic index 82.

NETHERLANDS.—*Northern Race* predominates. A brachy-cephalic element (index 83-87) occurs in the provinces of Noord-Holland and Zeeland.

GERMANY.—The *Northern Race* is paramount in the northern plains, and the *Alpine Race* prevails in the southern uplands; there is a decrease in dolichocephaly, blondness and height from north to south.

AUSTRIA-HUNGARY contains several racial elements :—

In AUSTRIA proper and Salzburg, traits of the *Northern Race* predominate. The cephalic index varies from 79 to 81, and blond types are frequent; the average stature is about 1·65m. to 1·67m. (5ft. 5in. to 5ft. 5¾in.). Elsewhere the cephalic index ranges from 83 to 86; darker types prevail; the stature in the east averages 1·62m. to 1·64m, (5ft. 3¾in. to 5ft. 4½in.). A tall type (Deniker's *Adriatic* or *Dinaric Race*) occurs in the south, the stature of which averages from 1·68m. to 1·72m. (5ft. 6in. to 5ft. 7¾in.); it is brachycephalic (index 81-86), and has dark hair and a narrow straight nose. Thus the Cevenole and Anatolian varieties of the *Alpine Race* are present in Austria.

HUNGARY.—The Magyars were originally of Finno-Ugrian origin (p. 49). The *Finno-Ugrian* type is brachycephalic or mesaticephalic, with projecting cheek-bones, straight or concave nose, yellowish white skin; straight brown hair, and short stature. The Magyars have, however, assimilated to a European type; their cephalic index is probably 84, they have a moderately dark colouring, and medium stature, 1·619m. to 1·646m. (5ft. 3¼in. to 5ft. 4¾in.).

EASTERN EUROPE :—

RUSSIA.—Three racial elements occur, the *Northern,*
Alpine, and *Ural-Altaian :—*

1. To the *Northern Race* belong the Letto-
Lithuanians, with a cephalic index 77-80, tall
stature, a long face, and fair colouring, 67% being
pure blonds.

2. To the *Alpine Race* belong the three main
groups of Russians :—

(i) The Great Russians in the north, east, and
centre are brachycephalic (index 82), with a
square face, heavy features, reddish blond hair,
orange-brown eyes, and a stature averaging
1·64m. (5ft. 4½in.).

(ii) The Little Russians in the south, on the
Black Mould belt, have a cephalic index of 82-83,
darker colouring, and taller stature.

(iii) The White Russians in the west, between
Poland and Lithuania, have a cephalic index of
82; they are the fairest of the three groups, and
are of medium height.

The Polesians of the Pinsk marshes, with a
cephalic index of 82-83; straight flaxen hair, and
short stature, 1·635m. (5ft. 4¼in.); constitute
Deniker's *Oriental Race.*

The Poles mainly belong to the *Alpine Race*; their
cephalic index varies from 80 in the west to 83 in
the east, they are moderately fair, and of very short
stature, 1·61m. (5ft. 3½in.). They belong to Deniker's
Vistulian Race.

3. Three branches of the *Ural-Altaian* are
represented :—

(i) To the *Mongols* belong the Kalmuks between
the Don and the Dnieper.

(ii) To the *Turki* belong the Kirghiz round the north and west of the Caspian Sea, the Volga Tatars to the east of Russia, and the Crimean Tatars to the south.

(iii) To various divisions of the *Ugrians* belong the Lapps and the Finns to the north-west, and the Samoyads and others to the north-east. Many of these groups have entirely lost their "Mongolian" character, *e.g.*, the Finns. The Finns as a whole are mesaticephalic (index 76-77) to brachycephalic (index 81-82). They are divisible into two main groups:—

(i.) The Karelians in the east are less brachycephalic, have chestnut hair, straight grey eyes, brown complexion, and are tall and slim.

(ii.) The Tavastians, in the west, are more brachycephalic, with light flaxen or tow-coloured hair, small and slightly oblique blue eyes, a white complexion, and are short, broad, and thick set.

BALKAN STATES.—Mixed peoples, mainly of *Alpine*, *Finno-Ugrian* and *Turki* origin, prevail in the Balkan States.

The Roumanians consist of *Turki* and Slav (*Alpine Race*) elements; the cephalic index ranges from 79 on the east coast to 85 in the west, rising in places to 87·8; with dark colouring, and a stature of 1·638m. (5ft. 4½in.). They speak a Romance language.

The Bulgarians contain *Ugrian* and Slav elements; their cephalic index is 78 on the coast, and 85 in the west; they have a broad, flattish face; black hair; small slant eyes; and a stature of 1·63m. (5ft. 4¼in.), with heavy figures. They speak a Slav language.

The Albanians are Southern Slavs; they are hyper-brachycephalic (index rising to 89), relatively blond, with a stature of 1·68m. (5ft. 6in.). Their language is derived from the old Illyrian, a proto-Aryan dialect. Deniker places them in his *Adriatic* or *Dinaric Race.*

The Turks are brachycephalic, with a cephalic index of 85-87, a cuboid head, elongated oval face, straight, somewhat prominent nose; yellowish white complexion; dark hair; and dark non-Mongoloid eyes; they are of moderately tall stature, 1·675m. (5ft. 6in.), with a tendency to obesity. Of *Turki* origin.

SOUTHERN EUROPE :—

GREECE.—The indigenous *Mediterranean Race* has been overlaid by the *Alpine Race*; cephalic index 81; smooth oval face, rather narrow and high; nose straight, thin, and high; uniformly dark hair and eyes; stature 1·626m. (5ft. 4in.).

ITALY.—The *Alpine Race* occurs in the basin of the Po, between the Apennines and the Alps; cephalic index 83-87; with fair to medium colouring, and often light brown hair and eyes; the stature averages 1·645m. (5ft. 4¾in.), but is taller towards the north. The *Mediterranean Race* occupies the peninsula; the cephalic index ranges from 84 in the north to 77-78 in the south; brunet types increase in frequency to over 60% in the south; and the stature falls to 1·55m. (5ft. 1in.) in the south. There are traces of the *Northern Race* in Lombardy.

SPAIN.—Mainly inhabited by the *Mediterranean Race*; the physical characters are fairly uniform. The cephalic index is pretty generally 76-79, but in the north-west mountains it is broader, 79-80; dark hair and eyes; the stature averages about 1·62m. to 1·66m. (5ft. 3¾in. to 5ft. 5in.), increasing from the centre towards the coast.

ASIA.

OUR knowledge of the history of Central and Northern Asia is very imperfect, and owing to the great movements of peoples that have taken place, the racial history is a peculiarly difficult problem. A further source of uncertainty is the indefinite manner in which racial terms have been employed. The following sketch, therefore, must be regarded as tentative.

The aboriginal population of Northern Asia belongs to that group to which the name *Ural-Altaic* is frequently applied. This term was designed to express linguistic affinities, and though the group extends beyond its geographical significance, it will be provisionally adopted, for want of a better designation. These people are also usually called *Mongols* or *Northern Mongols*. The term Mongol appears to have been originally given to a horde of aggressive nomads who were recruited from Turki, Oghuz and Tungus tribes. Latterly it has been so employed as to embrace all the brachycephalic, straight-haired peoples of Asia, who have a more or less yellowish skin, frequently high cheek-bones, and often a peculiar kind of eye, which may be also oblique.

The short, western, and northern *Ural-Altaians* form one division, which includes such peoples as the *Ugrians* (in part), *Palæasiatics*, some of the *Tungus*, and the true *Mongols*. The taller eastern Ural-Altaians include the *Manchu-Koreans*, but amongst these a race mixture may be suspected.   The Finno-Ugrians and Turki are of mixed descent.

In prehistoric times there appears to have been an extension of *dolichocephalic peoples* (a branch of which group occurred along the plains of Europe) right across Asia, of which the *Ainus* may be modified descendants, and whose influence may be detected among the Manchus and upper class Tungus. This presumed migration does not appear to have effected much in the way of civilisation; probably because the people were in a low stage of culture and lived under unfavourable conditions.

There was probably a later extension of *dolichocephals* more nearly related to the Nordic race of Europe. The Chinese annals tell of red-haired, blue-eyed tribes in Central Asia, of which the *Wusuns* were one, and recent excavations in Chinese Turkistan have demonstrated the former occurrence of this type in that region. They were of better physique and greater energy than the older dolichocephals, and appear to have belonged to that race which many ethnologists term Aryan, but Kingsmill* has

---

* " In the old Iranian cosmogony Feridun (Thraêtaona, the Vedic Traitona), had three sons, Çairima, Tuirya, and Airya, the eponyms respectively of the Çairimyans (Sauromats), Tuiryans (Turanians), i.e., the ancient inhabitants of the Pamirs and the basin of Eastern Turkistan, and the Aryans (these last forming, however, only one of the many families comprised by modern ethnologists under the general term Aryan). As Feridun is always in the Iranian legend the ' Athwyan,' i.e., the descendant of Athwya, I have suggested the term Athwyan to cover the entire section of the blond race now roughly known as Aryan, and would reserve the latter term for the first stream of the immigrants into India some eighteen centuries B.C. and their immediate relations, especially the Iranians."

(T. W. Kingsmill, *Jnl. China Branch Roy. Asiatic Soc.,* XXXVII, 1906, p. 35.)

proposed the term *Athwyan* for the Aryan group of peoples, and *Turanian* for this particular branch.

The *Finno-Ugrian* and *Turki* peoples may very well have arisen from a crossing between Ural-Altaians and Athwyans. This perhaps might help to account for the degree of culture arrived at by the Proto-Finns in their Asiatic home in Altai, and of that of the Hiung-nu and Uigurs.

A mixture of races has also occurred in South-eastern Asia. The yellow-skinned brachycephals, for whom Kingsmill proposes the name of *Pareæans*, are the *Indo-Chinese*, or *Southern Mongols*, of most authors. There is good evidence of an entirely distinct race, characterised by fine features, straight eyes, and probably a narrow head, inhabiting parts of Southern China, and it seems to have a wide range in that part of Asia. The *Man-tse* of Yun-nan and Se-chuen (who are described as tall, graceful, with a brownish but not yellow skin, the colour of the hair has a tendency to chestnut and is sometimes wavy, face oval, cheek-bones but slightly prominent, nose elevated and moderately broad, eyes large, level, with no fold of the upper eyelid), are descendants of this race, which is probably allied to the Indonesian stock.

The *Chinese* are Pareæan at base with other mixtures. Many students believe that the progressive element of the old Chinese civilisation was due to a migration of a semi-cultured people from Chinese Turkistan or even, originally, from further west. The *Japanese* are also Pareæans (Indo-Chinese) with a strong Korean blend, and in places with a substratum of Ainu blood.

The *Negrito* race must in early days have had a greater extension in the extreme south-east of Asia and in the East Indian Archipelago than occurs at present. The *Melanesians* have left no trace of their assumed ancient passage, except in the south of the Archipelago. The *Sakai*, the *Batin* of Sumatra and the *Toala* of Celebes have been recognised as belonging to the *Pre-Dravidian* race, and they may be regarded as being vestiges of the Australian migration. The existing population of the Archipelago, with exceptions just noted, consists mainly of varying degrees of mixture of dolichocephalic *Indonesians* with brachycephalic *Proto-Malays*. In some places there has also been a slight Arab influence; in others, Dravidians from India on the one hand and Chinese on the other have definitely modified the population.

The brachycephals south of the Himalayas are more closely related to the Tibetans than to the Indo-Chinese. Keane distinguishes three racial elements among the *Tibetans:*—The Bod-pa, the settled and more or less civilized section, who occupy most of the southern and more fertile provinces. The Dru-pa, peaceful, semi-nomadic pastoral tribes of the northern plateaus. The Tanguts, predatory tribes who hover about the north-eastern borderland.

The ethnological history of India is dealt with on pages 56-60.

The plateaus of Western Asia appear to have been originally inhabited by the *Alpine Race*. "Aryans," allied to the Aryas who entered North-east India, have over-lorded Persia, and for ages Turki tribes have poured

over the whole area from the north-east, and Semites
have encroached from the south, while the littoral of
Asia Minor has always been more or less occupied by
Mediterraneans. It is significant that the *Sumers*, who
founded the earliest Babylonian civilisation, were possibly
of Turki origin; they soon became Semitised, but the
civilisation was pre-Semitic.

Ural-Altaians.

Nearly the whole breadth of Central Asia, excluding
the deserts and mountains, is a grass-clad region in
which cattle-keeping is the natural industry. In the
inhospitable regions to the north, grass is replaced by
the lichen generally known as "reindeer moss."
Horses, sheep, goats, cows, and camels are kept in
the steppe region, while reindeer alone can exist on
the tundra. The latter region is inhabited by wandering
tribes who depend more or less on the reindeer for
their existence. The Lapps, and the tribes living in
the tundra of North Russia, are in a similar condition.
Both the steppe and the tundra necessitate a nomadic
life, and this fact has had a profound effect on the
history of Asia. The desiccation of Central Asia has
caused migration from lands that were formerly more
fertile, and this was facilitated by the mobile habits
of the pastoral peoples. The inroads of the hordes
of this origin into India, Western Asia, and Eastern
Europe have left a deep mark alike in racial distribution,
history, and tradition.

Herders on the Steppes.

The *Khalkas* are a good type of a purely nomadic people.

The only two modes of sustenance possible to them are hunting and herding, and these are facilitated by the fact that they possess the horse as a domestic animal. As a result of these occupations, the men are fine horsemen and extremely hardy; they are, however, prone to idleness. The women's work consists in milking twice daily, taking charge of the beasts at foaling time, house-work, needlework, the manufacture of household utensils, tanning leather, fulling wool, and making illuminant, soap, and dyes. All the labour of shifting the camp falls upon them.

In their organisation the unit is the family, and above this the sole grouping is the tribe, which is practically the union of families of common origin. Authority is vested in the old men, of whom the patriarch is chief; he combines the functions of father, teacher, magistrate, priest, and sovereign, being the depositary of traditions and the supreme judge. Otherwise there is essential equality between men. Children are numerous, and have a profound veneration for their father, from whom age does not enfranchise them. There is no government external to the family.

Property consists of cattle. There is no personal ownership of land otherwise than the temporary possession constituted by usage of it.

Shamanism is the basis of their religion, but it is overlaid by Buddhism. Filial piety characterises later religious developments.

Herders on the Tundra.

There are four groups of peoples living in the tundra :—

(1) The purely pastoral peoples who possess herds of domesticated reindeer and live on their milk and flesh— *Samoyads*, etc.

(2) The pastoral groups whose herds of reindeer are insufficient to support life. This may result from epidemics or from the cantonment system established by the Russian Government; the limitation of pasturing rights necessitates a reduction in the number of the reindeer, and the few that remain are too precious to be used for food. The means of subsistence have to be supplemented by hunting, fishing and trading—*Tungus, Yakuts*, etc.

(3) The peoples who possess the most numerous herds of reindeer of all the tundra tribes. These animals are not tame, they cannot be milked and are not of much use for transport, but they are bred in large numbers for food and trade—*Chukchis* and *Koryaks*.

(4) Those who have no reindeer and have to support a miserable existence by hunting, fishing and trading; they are often dependent on other groups—*Chukchis, Gilyaks*, and many remnants of other tribes.

The poverty of the soil and rapid exhaustion of the food necessitate frequent changes of pasturage. In winter the herds descend into the plains and valleys; in summer they retreat to the hills, partly to escape from the mosquitoes. Herders of reindeer lead a more wandering life than other pastors.   It is a poor living, ten reindeer giving only as much milk as one cow.

The Chukchis rarely have more than one wife, who is earned by working for her for a year or more in the camp of the prospective father-in-law.   The women are treated as equals, the children are well-behaved, and there is great family affection.   The poorer Ostyaks marry only one wife, but the rich look upon it as a right to have two or more.   Among them too the children are dutiful, and there is great family affection.   The Samoyad wife has equal   rights   with   her   husband   and   is   treated accordingly.

There is no government among the Chukchis and no chiefs other than the fictitious chiefs appointed by the Russians, who possess no power.   The people live in a state of anarchy, yet the greatest unanimity prevails.

When the Russian Government does not interfere the grazing grounds are open to all.   Reindeer constitute the real property; three hundred will suffice for a Lapp family, a Lapp with a herd of five thousand is a veritable capitalist; the poorest have only half-a-dozen.

Shamanism is prevalent throughout the district. The Coast Chukchis have no noteworthy religion ; among them there is no crime except that committed under the influence of liquor.   The Ostyaks believe that a dead man continues to lead a spirit life among the living; his reward is to do good, his punishment to do evil to his living relatives.   Many Samoyads are nominal Christians so long as things go well with them.

INDIA.

India broadly speaking is divided into three main geographical areas:—(1) the southern slopes of the Himalaya, inhabited by broad-headed peoples who possess most of the character described as "Mongolian;" (2) the valleys of the Indus and the Ganges; (3) the Deccan or central and southern tableland. These areas are inhabited by dolichocephalic peoples except for a group of brachycephalic peoples who extend in a broad band down the west coast of India from the lower waters of the Indus to about latitude 12° N.

The languages fall into three main divisions:— (1) Aryan (Sanskrit, Pali, and Prakit with its modern derivatives Hindi, Bengali, etc., and Sinhali). (2) Dravidian (Tamil, Telugu, Malayalim, etc.). (3) The Munda languages belong to the Mon-Khmer family. Schmidt calls this group of languages Austroasiatic, which with the Austronesian (Melanesian, Polynesian, Malay, etc.) form his Austric linguistic family.

When the *Aryas* entered India from the north-west, some 2,000 years B.C., they first occupied the fertile lands of the Punjab; their progress south-west being barred by the deserts of Rajputana they passed into the valleys of the Jumna and Ganges, where they found the Naga, yellow peoples who had a snake (cobra) cult. When they reached the Gandak they encountered the Dasyu, who were described as dark-coloured, low-statured, treacherous and foul in manners. The aboriginal elements were prepotent, and the so-called Aryan conquest was more social than ethnical, the spread of the culture was peaceful and intellectual rather than imposed by conquest (Crooke). The entry into the Punjab was a very gradual one, probably extending over centuries.

The *Sakas*, the Se (Sek) of the Chinese annals, originally were a horde of pastoral nomads, like the modern Turkomans, who came from the region between the Jaxartes (Syr Darya) and west of the country of the Wusuns (p. 49). About 150 B.C. they were expelled from their pasture grounds by another horde, the Yueh-chi, and compelled to migrate southwards. They ultimately reached India about 150-140 B.C., probably through the Pamirs, Gilgit and the Suwat Valley, until they entered the plains of Peshawar. Another branch advanced further to the south, perhaps crossed Sind, and occupied Kathiawar. Pahlavas from Persia and Yavanas ('Asiatic Greeks') also occupied parts of Western India about this time. A Turki-tribe, the *Yueh-chi*, who occupied lands in the province of Kan-suh in North-western China, were ousted between 174 and 160 B.C. by an allied horde, the Hiung-nu, and a multitude of from half a million to a million persons of all ages and both sexes migrated westward. They conquered the Wusuns and drove out the Sakas, whose land they occupied. About 140 B.C. the Hiung-nu and Wusuns drove them southwards to Sogdiana and Bactria, lands to the north and south of the Upper Oxus (Amu Darya). Here they became a settled nation. Kadphises I., chief of the Kushan section of the horde, established himself as sole monarch of the Yueh-chi nation about 45 A.D., and Kadphises II. extended his dominion about 90-100 A.D.

all over North-western India as far as Benares, but excluding Sind. The collapse of the Kushan power in India
occurred about 226 A.D. About 455 A.D. an irruption
of savage *Hunas* poured from the steppes of Central Asia
through the north-west passes and carried devastation
over the plains and crowded cities of India. They were
repulsed by Skandagupta, King of the Gupta Empire, but
the latter succumbed in 470 to fresh invasions of these
White Huns (Ephthalites, Huna, Hoa, or Ye-the), a
brachycephalic polyandric Tatar people. They were
expelled about 528 A.D. by a confederation of Hindu
princes. The arrival of the Turks in the Oxus valley
in the middle of the sixth century changed the
situation completely, and about 565 A.D. the White
Huns were destroyed and the Turks annexed the
whole of the remaining Hun empire. The *Gurjaras*
probably entered India about the same time as
the White Huns and settled in large numbers in
Rajputana. It is not known whence they came. They
formed kingdoms in early mediaeval times, and many
kings of the powerful Kanauj dynasty were Gurjaras.
The surviving Gujars are primarily a pastoral people,
though largely engaged in agriculture. (Vincent A.
Smith.)

According to Risley there exists in the Kashmir Valley,
Punjab and Rajputana, a definite physical type represented by the Rajputs and Jats. This type possesses a
dolichocephalic head, straight, finely-cut, leptorrhine
nose, long, narrow face, well-developed forehead, regular
features, tall stature, and light transparent brown skin.
The Rajputs look upon governing and bearing arms as

the proper business of life. No regard is paid to educa-
tion. They are never artisans, and rarely trade. Caste
is not rigid, all Rajputs being theoretically, but not actually, of one blood. Widows may not remarry. They are
orthodox Hindus with ancestor worship. The Jat is a
sturdy, independent, patient husbandman, peaceable if
unmolested. Those of the western plains are pastors. The
Jats allow widows to remarry. They are Muhammadans
in religion.

Even the Rajputs cannot claim to be pure Aryans, and
the most ancient clans prove to be very mixed in origin.
In the Punjab we have reigning Brahman families which
became Rajput; in Oudh, Brahmans, Bhars and Ahirs
have all contributed to the Rajput clans, but the majority
appear to have been Aryanised Sudras. Of the clans of
Rajputana some—like the Chauhans, Solankis and
Gehlots—have a foreign origin; others are allied to the
Indo-Scythic Jats and Gujars; others represent ancient
ruling families with more or less probability. These
clans, however, acquired a certain homogeneity by constant intermarriage and the adoption of common customs
(J. Kennedy). The well-known clan of Parihar Rajputs
is a branch of the Gurjara or Gujar stock. Most of the
great Rajput clans are descended from foreign immigrants
of the fifth or sixth century A.D., or from indigenous
races such as the Gonds, Bhars, Kols, and the like.
(V. A. Smith.)

As soon as the Aryas established themselves in the
plains of the Ganges and Jumna, they mingled with the
aborigines, and by stress of the contact caste was
evolved, the Code of Manu written, and the elaborate

orthodox ritual built up. Thus was produced the mixed type of Hindustan and Bihar, with all grades of mixture, the Aryo-Dravidians of Risley. There are three divisions: The *Babhans* of Bihar, a fine manly people with Aryan type of features, medium height; they are mesaticephalic and mesorrhine. The territorial exogamous groups render it probable that they are a branch of the Rajputs. They are settled agriculturists, but will not drive the plough with their own hands.

The *Chamars* of the United Provinces and Bengal have been largely recruited from non-Aryan elements. They are of low medium stature, dolichocephalic and platyrrhine. They are leather workers and day-labourers. Polygyny is discouraged. They are a proud and punctilious people, but are looked upon as impure because they eat beef, pork, and fowls, and keep pigs. The *Brahmans* of the United Provinces are a dolichocephalic, mesorrhine people of medium height.

A zone of relatively *broad-headed* people extends from the great grazing country of the Western Punjab through the Deccan to the Coorgs. Risley supports the view that this may be the track of the Scythians, who found their progress east blocked by the Indo-Aryans and so turned south, mingled with the Dravidian population, and became the ancestors of the Marathas and Canarese. But evidence seems to be lacking that the " Scythians " penetrated far into the Deccan, and apart from brachycephaly there is little to associate these peoples with Scythians. It seems quite possible that these brachycephals are the result of an unrecorded migration of some members of the Alpine race from the highlands of South-west Asia in pre-historic times.

The main element in the modern *Mahrattas* (Marathas) is that known as Kunbi or Kurmi, a widespread caste of cultivators, undoubtedly of "Dravidian" (aboriginal) origin, numerous throughout the northern plains as far east as Bengal. The Mahrattas form the higher status group of this people, to which they have attained by the same methods as those of the Rajputs in the Punjab. Even now the difference between the Mahratta and Kunbi is mainly social. Hinduism prevails, though totems still survive.

Three other members of this group are: The *Prabhus*, a mesaticephalic, mesorrhine people of rather low stature, who reside chiefly in the districts around Bombay City, but who originally came from Oudh; probably the Gupta dynasty belonged to this stock. The original occupation was that of the soldier, now they wield the pen. Polygyny is allowed but is not the rule; neither divorce nor remarriage of widows are allowed. They follow the Vedic form of religion, but arms and writing materials are worshipped. The *Canarese* are mesaticephalic with regular features. They are frank, independent, intelligent, and fond of show. Formerly they made wide-ranging forays, adopting guerilla methods; they were unscrupulous with friend or foe, and too individualistic to build up a kingdom. The former fighting middle class now cultivate the soil. Every family has its guardian or symbol, which was formerly a totem. The *Coorgs*, who inhabit the extreme south of the Bombay Presidency, and speak a Dravidian language, are a mesaticephalic, mesorrhine people, of medium height, with light brown skin and straight hair. They are agriculturists with sporting and fighting proclivities, and are the finest people in South India,

The pure *Veddas* of Ceylon are probably the least modified survivals of the ancient *Pre-Dravidian* race; they are a grave but happy people, with a love of liberty, upright, hospitable, and quiet. Lying and theft are unknown among them; they have a great fear of strangers. They live in rock shelters or simple huts, and subsist by hunting and collecting honey, etc. After a death they perform certain dances and rites through a shaman to the recently departed spirit, and they also propitiate certain powerful spirits, male and female, by sacrifices and ceremonial dances. They are strictly monogamous, and live in detached communities which have no regular chief. Some of the Pre-Dravidian tribes of South India are jungle hunters in a state of savagery, with very little, if any, agriculture; others are agriculturists, while some are artisans. Some are monogamous, others polygynous. Animism is very widely spread, but simple forms of Hinduism have been adopted by the more cultured tribes.

Various stages of culture are met with among the true *Dravidian* peoples. Some, like the totemic *Bhils* of the north-west Deccan, live mainly on natural produce, but even these are taking to agriculture. The Bhils, the outcasts of centuries, are contemned by the Hindus and scorned by the Rajputs; but when a Rajput chief is installed, it is the despised Bhil who puts the sign of kingship on his forehead,

Southern India is mainly inhabited by numerous Dravidian peoples who are grouped linguistically into Telegu, Tamil, and Malayalim. The *Telegu* (Telinga, Kalinga, or Klings) extend over the Coromandel coast, the northern half of the Madras Presidency, and Hyderabad. Thurston has recently shown that the Telegu of the north-east have an average cephalic index of about seventy - eight, showing that so-called "Scythian" mixture has taken place. The Telegus have superior physique to the Tamils and are lighter in colour. Formerly they possessed a martial spirit, founded famous kingdoms, and sent colonists to the East; now the Madrasi is a man of peace, an agriculturist and shopkeeper. The *Tamils* occupy most of the southern half of Madras Presidency and the north of Ceylon. The *Nayars* form the bulk of the Sudra population of Malabar. They are described as frank, affectionate, hospitable, industrious, with reverence for authority. They are not strict vegetarians. Malabar is the most literate country in all India, and almost every Nayar girl goes to school. These people were the swordsmen, the military caste of the west coast of India. There are numerous divisions which may or may not be endogamous, but the mother-right kinship groups (Taravad) are strictly exogamous. Very young girls are married symbolically with a ceremony at which the Tali is tied; the true marriage to another man is a simple affair. In South Malabar the woman never lives in her husband's house, but she does so in North Malabar; the relations between the sexes are not influenced by considerations of property. A good deal of license is allowed by some groups, others are strictly monogamous; polyandry certainly occurred formerly, as it still does amongst other Malabar castes. In Malabar the most abstract religion of South India is mingled with the most primitive; serpent worship occurs. The *Todas* of the Nilgiri Hills are somewhat aberrant. They are strong, agile, intelligent, dignified, and cheerful. They are fully clothed, and are without weapons. They live a simple pastoral life and are concerned solely with the care of the dairy. They form a typical polyandrous community; when a woman marries it is understood that she becomes the wife of her husband's brothers (own or clan). Recently there is a tendency for polyandry to be associated with polygyny. Descent is patrilineal with few traces of mother-right. "It is doubtful whether crime can be said to exist among the Todas, they have a code of offences against the dairy, but these must be considered as sins rather than as crimes" (Rivers). Gods once believed to be active and living among men have become shadowy beings; there is no proof that the buffalo was ever regarded as a god; ritual has killed the spirit of religion and in its turn is becoming perfunctory. Corpses are burnt.

The *Munda-speaking* peoples are a very ancient element in the population and appear to have been the original inhabitants of the valley of the Ganges in Western Bengal; after many wanderings they settled mainly in Chota Nagpur. Everywhere they have been more or less modified by the Dravidians, and while scattered relics of the languages are preserved, the original physical type appears to have been assimilated to that of the Dravidians, but perhaps it was originally a closely-allied type.

They may belong to the primitive Indonesian race. The more important tribes are the *Mundas, Bhumij, Ho, Juangs*, etc. Most are divided into exogamous septs, probably originally totemic. There is a vague supreme sun-god; human sacrifices were once offered. Memorial stones are erected.

In Western Bengal the " Dravidian " element is more prominent in the population, but this is modified towards the east, and in Eastern Bengal Mongoloid characters predominate. The latter are the " Mongolo-Dravidians " of Risley. The majority of the people are agricultural.

ASSAM.

From very early times inhabitants of India proper migrated into the rich alluvial plains of Assam, many of whom mixed with the aboriginal population to form the "semi-Hinduized aborigines." Muhammadans are also especially numerous in the plains south of the Khasi hills. The Hinduized *Meithis* or *Manipuri* are a mixed people sprung from the Kukis in the south, the Nagas in the north, and Shan and Burmese in the east.

The first *Indo-Chinese* invasion appears to have been by Tibeto-Burmans. At the end of the 8th Century A.D. the *Shans* began to conquer Assam. King Chukupha (A.D. 1228) assumed for himself and people the name of Aham, the peerless; this is now softened to Assam. His successor adopted the Hindu religion, and the Aham Shans grew to be regarded as a new division of the Hindu Assamese population. This dynasty was overthrown in 1810 by the Burmese; when various branches of the Tai or Shan stock, such as the Khamtis, Phakis and Kamjangs, came into the country. The *Ahams* or *Hindu Assamese* are a strong, healthy race, now mostly poor cultivators; they are generally tall, and lighter than the Bengalis, with a flat face, high cheek bones, black and coarse hair, and scanty beard; they are divided into castes; they bury their dead.

The hills were occupied by the British to protect the plains from the raids of the hill-tribes, who, from an ethnological point of view, form the most interesting section of the people.

The *Lusheis* (sometimes called *Kukis*) of the Lushai Hills are a short Mongoloid people; who live in villages under an independent chief, but the people are very democratic. Rice is seldom cultivated on the same land two years running. The villages, which are on the tops of hills, are frequently removed. The houses are built on piles. There is a large house for young men and guests. They are only head-hunters incidentally. They believe in a supreme being, but the numerous spirits are more important.

The *Khasis* of the Khasi Hills are distinctly Mongoloid. An immense number of exogamous septs, some totemic. Mother-right obtains, and males can own only self-acquired property. They worship ancestors, natural forces, and deities. Monoliths are often erected as cenotaphs, and there are numerous other stone erections. Their language belongs to the Mon-Khmer family, and is closely allied to the Palaung-Wa dialects of Burma.

The *Nagas* " more closely resemble the natives of the

Malayan Archipelago than any of the other races inhabiting the hills or plains of India and Assam " (Furness). The villages are on hill tops, with no marked tribal unity. Each village is divided into endogamous groups (khel) which contain several exogamous septs, but the latter may be scattered through several villages. Each khel (except among the Sema and Angami tribes) has its bachelors' house. Descent is reckoned through the father. They are monogamous. All are head-hunters. Mother-right obtains among the Garos and Kukis.

The *Chingpos* or *Singphos* arrived in Assam from the east of the upper waters of the Irawadi about 1793 A.D. They are the same people as the Chingpaw, Kachin or Kakhyen of North Burma, with tawny yellow to brown complexions, and marked Mongolian features. For several generations they were the terror of the country, carrying off people into slavery. Polygyny prevails. They have a confused notion of a supreme being, but propitiate only three malignant spirits or nhats.

The *Mishmis* of the extreme north-east are constantly on the move in their trading expeditions. They attend to cultivation less than their neighbours, and count riches by the number of their half-wild cattle and their wives; the cattle are not used for agricultural purposes or for milk. Some have " almost Aryan features," and they are probably allied to the *Man-tse*, a pre-Chinese people of South China, who originally came from the west.

BURMA.

The original population may be represented by the *Selung*, the nomadic fishers of the Mergui Archipelago, who have no fixed villages and do not cultivate the soil. The men are below average size, vary from light to dark brown, and have long, lank black hair. They are regarded as being of *Indonesian* race, but there seems to be a *Proto-Malay* mixture.

All the other peoples belong to the *Indo-Chinese* population and are grouped into *Mon-Khmer, Tibeto-Burman* and *Siamese-Chinese* sub-families. Probably 2,000-3,000 years ago the coast was occupied by Indonesians and the interior by tribes speaking Mon-Khmer languages. From the North came the ancestors of the Tibeto-Burman and Tai peoples, who within the last fifteen centuries have flooded Indo-China with successive swarms of conquerors and have received through Mon and Khmer channels a varnish of Indian civilisation.

Some believe that the *Mon* were the earlier settled race to whom the *Talaing (Telinga* or *Klings)* brought a civilisation from India about 1,000 B.C. The fused race is now known by either name. In dress and customs they resemble the Burmans. To this group belong the peaceful, avaricious, sanctimonious *Palaung* of the Shan States; and the *Wa* tribes of the north-east frontier, who are brave, energetic, independent, unmercenary. The dark wild Wa are prosperous headhunters, who collect skulls as a protection against evil spirits, and are not habitual cannibals. The poor tame Wa are lighter in colour.

The earliest seat of the *Tibeto-Burman* speaking peoples appears to have been the head-waters of the Yang-tse-Kiang. There is no proof that the *Burmans* reached the Irawadi Valley before 600 B.C. In the ninth century A.D. Burmans occupied the greater part of Upper Burma and the Mon were on the lower Irawadi, Sitang, and Salwin (the Khmer were then at the height of their power, with magnificent towns and temples in Cambodia). In the fourteenth century A.D. the *Tai* moved from Tali, overran North Burma and forced the Burmans down on the Mons. After much fighting, with varying successes, the Burmans merged with the Mons in the sixteenth century. The *Burmans* have marked Mongoloid characters. They are the most engaging race in the east, the men are unbusinesslike and courteous, with a great sense of humour, great pride of race and self-reliance, brave, but not fool-hardy. The Burmese nature is so essentially democratic that there is no indigenous caste system. The Burman is essentially an agriculturalist, but is lazy; they dress in brilliant colours. They live chiefly on rice with a few condiments and drink water. Their houses are of wood or bamboo and raised on posts; but have masonry pagodas and temples. There are very numerous monasteries. The Burmans most nearly of all Buddhists follow the teaching of Buddha. No Burman is considered a human being till he has put on the yellow robe for a longer or shorter period; but their Buddhism is superficial, it being superimposed on an earlier and still strong belief in spirits (*nats*); and animism prevails everywhere.

The *Chingpaw*, *Chingpo*, *Kakhyen*, or *Kachin* of the extreme north are constantly moving southwards. They

are pugnacious, vindictive, stiff-necked people, with a
constant tendency to disintegration. The Chingpaw
exhibit two types: one markedly Mongoloid, the other
"much finer, with regular Caucasic features, long oval
face, pointed chin, aquiline nose" (Keane).

The Siamese-Chinese linguistic group comprises Tai
or Shan, and the Karens. The *Tai* first appear in history
in Yun-nan, south-west China, and early, small swarms of
them entered Burma 2,000 years ago; the foundation of
the Tai principalities in the Salwin Valley took place
about the third century A.D.; a great wave of immigra-
tion occurred in the sixth century; they peopled the Shan
States. When the 'Mongol' hordes under Kublai Khan
in the latter half of the thirteenth century conquered
Indo-China, the Tai went westward and supplied kings to
North Burma for two centuries. The *Shans* of Eastern
Burma resemble the Burmans, but are fairer, mild and
good-humoured; technically are fervent Buddhists.
Their tendency has always been to fritter away their
strength, as are always swarming. The *Karen* clans were
driven south from China by the Tai, and later were
driven back into the hills of the south-east by the Mons
and the Burmans. There are two types, the White and
Red Karens; sturdy race, straight black and brownish
hair, black and hazel eyes; "here also a Caucasic strain
may be suspected" (Keane).

THE NEGRITOES OF ASIA.

Flower regards them "as representing an infantile,
undeveloped, or primitive form of the type from which
the African Negroes on the one hand, and the Melane-

sians on the other, with all their various modifications, may have sprung up."

Andamanese.

The inhabitants of the Andaman Islands were said to be formerly virtuous, modest, honest and frank. Conjugal fidelity was the absolute rule, and divorce was formerly unknown. The women are on a footing of equality with the men and do their full share of work. The Andamanese have a sense of humour. They express any emotion whether of joy or sorrow by loud weeping.

They live mainly on fish, wild yams, turtle, pig and honey. Their food is mostly eaten cooked. The men are hunters and collectors and do not till the soil, nor do they keep domestic animals. The men go nude, the women wear a small leaf apron ; both sexes wear a number of ornaments.

They live in small encampments round an oval dancing ground, their huts being constructed of branches and leaves. Bows and arrows are used for hunting and fishing ; all their original implements were made of wood, bone or shell. They make canoes some of which have outriggers, but they never venture far from the shore. Pottery is made by the men.

There is no organised polity in the Andamanese community. There is generally one man who excels the rest in hunting, warfare, wisdom, and kindliness, and he is deferred to and becomes in a sense chief. A regular feature of Andamanese social life is the meeting at intervals between two or more communites. Marriage is strictly monogamous.

The Andamanese have a system of taboos on certain foods, notably turtle and pig, at those periods of life which they regard as critical. Disease and death are attributed to the spirits of jungle and sea, and after a death has taken place the camping place will be abandoned for a fresh site. The Andamanese religious system is exceedingly primitive. There are certain spirits of sea and jungle whom they must avoid vexing; chief of these is Biliku who controls the weather. Biliku is generally regarded as feminine and the north-east wind belongs to her, while her male counterpart Tarai owns the south-west wind. The spirits of the dead are believed by some tribes to haunt the jungle or the sea, and by others to repair to a place below the earth where there is a jungle.

Semang of the Malay Peninsula.

The Semang are a nomadic people living by collecting and hunting; the wilder ones will often not remain longer than three days in one place. Very few have taken to agriculture. Their clothing consists of a girdle of leaves or a loin-cloth of tree bark. Their distinctive weapon is the bow with poisoned arrows. They are strictly monogamous and both sexes are faithful.

There is a chief of each tribe who acts as chief medicine-man and exercises authority like the head of a family. All men are on an equal footing. Crime is rare; theft is punished by a fine. All property is held in common. Barter in jungle produce is carried on with the Malays.

A child is named after the tree near which it is born, the fruit of that tree being taboo to it. They have no great fear of the ghosts of the deceased. They have vague kind of deities, but there is no trace of an actual cult. They recognise the thunder god, Kari, who is the creator of most things and the judge of men.

The *Aket (Orang Raket)*, eastern of Sumatra, are closely allied to the Semang (Moszkowski).

Aetas of the Philippines.

The Aetas or Aitas are an indolent, timid and peaceful people, but become fierce and violent under provocation. They are somewhat inclined to be mischievous and thievish. They are fond of music and dances. They live mainly on game, fish, wild honey and forest products.

One tribe file the front teeth to a point. Both men and women are scarified in certain parts of the body, but not tattooed. Various ornaments are worn. The women have bamboo combs thrust into their hair; these are decorated with scratch-work patterns, and often plumes of hair and coloured feathers are attached to these. The men often wear circlets of boars' bristles round their calves. The normal dress of the men and boys is a perineal band of bark or cloth, that of the women a short skirt of the same.

They are nomadic in habits, and live in rapidly constructed huts with roofs of leaves or grass, beneath which will perhaps be sleeping platforms of poles. Their weapons are bows with poisoned arrows, and lances. They wander about in bands of fifty or more. Monogamy is the general rule, but polygyny may be indulged in if an individual has sufficient wealth. The dead are buried in the ground with more or less elaborate ceremonies.

MALAY PENINSULA.

In the north of the Malay Peninsula peoples of Indo-Chinese extraction prevail; in the south three distinct races are represented: *Negrito* (Semang), *Pre-Dravidian* (Sakai), and *Indo-Chinese* (Malay).

The *Semang* have already been described. The *Sakai* or *Senoi* are largely nomadic, their agriculture being of the most primitive description, for which they usually employ a digging-stick; they frequently live in tree-huts or other temporary shelters. Men still wear the tree-bark loincloth and the women a tree-bark wrapper, but now both frequently wear Malay clothing. Their distinctive weapon is the blow pipe, which they have brought to a great perfection. They are strict in the observance of the marriage tie. They have the greatest possible fear of death, or rather of the ghost of the deceased, and seem to have a kind of deity.

A third main element in the southern portion of the Malay Peninsula is that comprised by the 'Savage Malays' or *Jakun*, many of which have mixed with Semangs and Sakais. They may be grouped under *Orang Bukit* (Land people) and *Orang Laut* (Sea people). Their skin is darker and their stature slightly shorter than that of the true Malays. They are largely nomadic, though the Land Jakun usually practise some form of agriculture; their clothing is like that of the Malays but scantier; they file their teeth but do not circumcise. The universal weapon of the jungle tribes is the blow-pipe with poisoned darts. The small huts are built on piles. They trade jungle produce with the Malays who oppress

them. The Orang Laut are nomadic fishers, who occasionally live in temporary huts built on the ground, when
they have occasion to build boats, mend nets, or collect
dammar, etc. The Jakun, unlike the Malay, is hospitable
and generous; childlike, and proud, he hates and fears
the Malay, though he has to trade with him. The
Malays despise and fear the Jakun, and attribute to them
supernatural power and an unlimited knowledge of the
secrets of nature. The Jakun acknowledge a supreme
being, but are pagans, and devoutly believe in hantu
(spirits and demons).

The true *Malay*, who call themselves *Orang Malayu*,
speak the standard, but quite modern, Malay language,
and are all Muhammadans. Originally they were an
obscure tribe who rose to power in the Menangkabau
district, Sumatra, not before the twelfth century, and
whose migrations date only from about the year 1160 A.D.
(Keane). At this time Singapore was founded by them,
when they professed some form of Hinduism; they were
converted to Islam about the middle of the thirteenth
century. The Malay is naturally of an easy-going,
indolent character, deliberate, reserved and taciturn.
The upper classes are exceedingly courteous, yet with
this outward refinement they have the most pitiless
cruelty and contempt of human life. They are false,
wily, and very frugal. 'The patriotism, self-respect,
reverence for immemorial law, loyalty to their rulers,
traditions of courtesy and love of study for its own sake
—things that contain the germ of national progress'
are admirable (Wilkinson). Nominally they are Moslems
of the Sunnite sect, but lack the fanaticism of that

religion; owing to their conservatism they are unwilling to give up any cult that they can possibly retain under a Muhammadan disguise, their demonology being made up of the strata of several successive religions.

BORNEO.

The natives of Borneo may be taken as a fair example of the distribution of races in the East Indian Archipelago, although, naturally, the conditions vary in different islands.

So far as our present knowledge goes, apart from obvious foreigners, there are only two races in Borneo, the dolichocephalic *Indonesian* and the brachycephalic *Proto-Malay*, but these are so intermixed that no tribe or people can be considered as a pure representative of either. The skin colour of the Borneans may be described as buff, in some quite light, in others light brown. The hair is usually wavy, and black with a reddish tinge. The stature varies from 1.42m. (4ft. 8in.) to 1.73m. (5ft. 8in.) the average being about 1.555m. (5ft. 1¼in.). The cephalic index falls into two groups, 70-79 and 80-89.

Scattered all over the interior, in the dense jungle, are the nomadic hunters, the *Punans, Bakatans, Ukits,* etc. The few wants of these mild and unwarlike savages are supplied by barter from friendly settled peoples. They are low brachycephals and may represent an aboriginal population.

There are numerous, scattered, usually weak tribes, such as the Land Dayaks, Malanau, Kalabit, Dusun, and Murut, who, taken as a whole, are dolichocephals.

They cultivate the soil, and are an amiable people, though given to head-hunting. The name *Kalamantan* has been given to this group of tribes.

Occupying the more favourable inland country is the *Kenyah-Kayan* group, average cephalic index 80. They are a very energetic people who are extending their sway. They are well organised, have powerful chiefs, and smelt iron. They also are head-hunters.

The *Iban*, or *Sea Dayaks* were originally a small coastal tribe, but through their truculence they have spread inland; they are slightly darker than the inland people and have average cephalic index 83. Although essentially an agricultural people, they are warlike, and passionately devoted to head-hunting. It is probable that the Iban belongs to the same stock as the true Malay and his migration into Borneo may be regarded as the first wave of the movement that culminated in the Malay Empire.

With the exception of the first group, all these peoples are agriculturists, living mainly on rice, which is usually grown on dry ground, but swamp rice is grown in the lowlands. They hunt all land animals which serve as food, and are fond of fish. They all live in long communal houses situated on the banks of the rivers. Some weave cotton cloths, those of the Iban being particularly beautiful. All are artistic. Their languages belong to the Indonesian group of the Austro-Asiatic division of the Austric family of languages.

All their actions are regulated by omen animals, most of which are birds, who are possessed with the spirit of certain invisible beings above and bear their names, but the gods themselves are vague owing to the importance of their messengers. The Iban believe in individual spirit-helpers.

The true *Malays* probably emigrated from the Malay Peninsula, they never penetrated into the interior, but certain coastal people have partly absorbed the Malay culture, spirit, and religion.

The *Chinese* have long traded in Borneo, but they do not appear to have materially modified the population. Western Borneo has, however, been affected by the *Indo-Javanese* civilisation.

So far as is known there is no indication in Borneo of a *Negrito* population, such as occurs in the Philippines and the Malay Peninsula, nor of a Vedda-like (*Pre-Dravidian*) element, such as P. Sarasin has recently found among Toala in Celebes, and Moszkowski among the Batin of Sumatra.

AMERICA.

It is a very difficult matter, with the facts at our disposal, to make a satisfactory classification of the American Indians, or Amerinds as they are sometimes termed. Usually the various peoples are grouped on a linguistic basis, but this system breaks down in California, where a large number of linguistic stocks are recognised without, however, there being a corresponding variation in physical type. A classification based on physical characters has already been given (pages 18, 19), but it also is unsatisfactory. A third method is based on geographical areas; this is convenient from a cultural point of view, and for lack of anything better this arrangement is provisionally adopted.

North America.

On geographical and cultural grounds the Indians of North America may be divided into the following groups:

I.—Eskimo.

II.—Tribes of the north Pacific coast.

III.—Tribes of the northern interior (the Mackenzie River basin and the high plateaus).

IV.—Tribes of the lower Pacific coast (Columbia River and California).

V.—Tribes of the great plains.

VI.—Northern and southern tribes of the eastern woodlands.

VII.—Tribes of the south-west and of Mexico.

Eskimo or Innuits.

The Eskimo are free, independent, happy, and extremely gentle in character; wrangling and fighting are unknown among them. Crimes, if committed, go unpunished. Their women are treated as equals,

They are essentially a littoral people, living primarily on sea mammals; reindeer and other animals are hunted; vegetable diet is inconsiderable. The whole community shifts its locality according to the season. In winter the houses of the northern and eastern tribes are hemispherical in form and built of snow, in summer of skins. The winter houses of the western Eskimo are of logs covered over with earth. Their clothes consist of skins, and they make use of dog-sledges and skin canoes constructed on bone or wooden frameworks. They are clever carvers in bone and ivory and illustrate daily events by engravings on bone, and the Aleutian Islanders in particular excel in basketry. They are extremely musical.

The social organisation is based on the immediate family. Polygyny and polyandry occur though monogamy is the rule. The people group together in villages, but there is no sort of recognised authority; custom is the only law. All property, except clothes, hunting appliances, and sewing implements of the women, is the common possession of one or at most three families. Personal property generally descends to the eldest son, who is bound to provide for the rest of the family; among the western Eskimo it is divided among the children, the youngest son receiving the best weapons.

ESKIMO.

Plate IX.]   [*Races of Man, p.* 80.

In religion shamanism is the rule, with a belief in guardian and hostile spirits. The shaman is termed "angekok," and may be of either sex. One spirit tends to predominate and to become the centre of the mythology. The western Eskimo attach great importance to the shades of deceased friends and also of animals.

North Pacific Tribes.

All the North Pacific tribes live by fishing; river salmon and deep-sea fish are caught. Many are also hunters, and the women collect roots and berries. They make use of dug-outs, and their tackle consists of fish-hooks, spears, nets and lines. They build houses of cedar planks with roofs of bark, and part of the year is passed in permanent villages. Their industries are based largely on the yellow and red cedar. They have simple basketry, and stone implements, which are not chipped, and are frequently made of slate. Their decorative art is highly conventionalised and very characteristic.

The *Tlingit* and *Haida* are divided into two exogamous moieties, the *Tsimshian* into four groups, which are to a limited extent totemic. The sub-groups are local, originally exogamic village communities of mainly matrilineal blood relatives. This system is less rigid among the southern peoples. Among the *Kwakiutl* a child belongs by blood to both father's and mother's family, but descent is practically matrilineal; clan-legend and crest constitute title to property for men, and these are not inherited but acquired by marriage. The village communities are mainly exogamic. There are four classes of society—chiefs, nobles, common people, and

slaves. During the summer months society is organised
on a totemic sept system; during the winter ceremonial
season the place of the sept is taken by a number of
societies, namely the groups of all those individuals upon
whom the same or almost the same power or secret has
been bestowed by one of the spirits.

They have a highly developed system of barter of which
the blanket is now the unit of value, formerly the units
were elk-skins, canoes and slaves; certain symbolic
objects have attained fanciful values. A vast credit
system has grown up, based on the custom of loaning
property; the festival at which this occurs is called
" potlatch."

The religion of these peoples is bound up with their belief
in animal helpers. Supernatural aid is given by the spirits
to those who win their favour. The Kwakiutl believe
their clans to have been founded by ancestors who had
certain relations with supernatural beings and obtained
from them crests, names, dances, etc. These spirits are
supposed to visit the people every year.

The raven is the chief figure in the mythology of this
region; he regulates the phenomena of nature, procures
fire, daylight and freshwater, and teaches men the arts.
In some places the mink assumes this rôle, or the bluejay.

Indians of the Northern Interior, or Athapascans.

These tribes are more correctly termed *Déné*. The
northern Déné are timid, cowardly, honest, and formerly
chaste; the southern are more manly. All are by neces-
sity hunting and fishing peoples, but the northern tribes
are among the most primitive of all American stocks.

These make rude pottery and weave a sort of cloth. The eastern Déné are patrilineal, nomad hunters, who gather berries and roots. The western are semi-sedentary owing to the abundance of salmon; they are divided into exogamous, matrilineal, totemic clans. There is a belief in guardian spirits, and shamanism obtains. The mythology almost always refers to a "transformer" who visited the world when incomplete and set things in order.

Tribes of the Pacific Coast.

The *Salish* tribes are closely allied to the Athapascans. The coastal Salish have abundance of fish, especially salmon; they have reached considerable prosperity and are lavish in their display of wealth. The advantage of location and facility of communication by canoes enabled them to become relatively civilised, as is shown by their social organisation with its rigid castes, their village life, secret societies and greater skill in decorative art.

The plateau Salish are more democratic, less settled, and more individualistic in religious matters than the coastal. The previous totemism is largely replaced by a belief in supernatural helpers, personifications of 'sulia,' or that mystery which prevades North American religion. The system of obtaining supernatural aid is more developed on the coast, where the 'sulia' becomes hereditary in families, and its emblem persists as the family crest.

The Californian tribes fall, both culturally and linguistically into three groups, of which the central is much the largest, the culture of that area being more general in type. These tribes are characterised by their use of the acorn for food and the absence of the canoe. The chief tribe of this group, the *Maidu*, practises an annual ceremony of "burning," when the property of those who have died within the past five years is destroyed so that the articles may pass to the spirit world for use by the owner. The north-western and south-western groups are mainly differentiated from the central by their dependence on fish for food, and by the extensive use of the canoe.

South of the Salish, and east of the Californian areas lie the *Shahaptian* and the vast *Shoshonean* tracts of country, the latter extending to the coast in the south of California. The culture of these peoples is distinguished by an extremely loose social organisation, lack of elaborate ceremonials, a completely different style of art, and, possibly, a mythology rather resembling that of the tribes of the east than the north-west coast type (Farrand).

The Lower Californians belong to the *Yuman* family; they are a collecting people of very low stage of cultural and linguistic development.

The *Seri* of north-west Mexico are the least advanced and most isolated tribe in North America. Their most esteemed virtue is shedding alien blood, and their blackest crime is alien marriage. Mother-right obtains perhaps to a greater extent than in any known people, and it is only in the chase or on the war-path that men come to the front. Polygyny prevails. The tribe is composed of exogamic, matrilineal, totemic clans. Most of their food is eaten raw; they do not cultivate the soil, and the dog is the only domestic animal. Their houses are flimsy huts. They make pottery, and rafts of canes. Bows and arrows are extensively used; there is no knife.

Tribes of the Great Plains.

These tribes contain representatives of various stocks, but chiefly Siouan, Caddoan or Pawnee, Algonquian and Kiowan. The *Sioux* may serve as typical. They were a free and dominant race of hunters and warriors, necessarily strong and active. Their habits centred round the buffalo, which provided the staple materials of nutrition and industry. The dog was domesticated before the horse was acquired in the eighteenth century. They also made use of nuts, berries and roots for food, but did not cultivate the soil to any extent. Their houses consisted of tent-shaped huts of saplings covered with brush, bark or skins when in the woodlands; on the plains earth lodges were built for winter, and tipis, or tents of long poles covered with skin, or in later times canvas, for summer. Their weapons were tomahawk, club, flint knife, and bow and arrow; they were made of stone, wood, bone and horn. Rude pottery and basketry were made but wood and skins were the raw materials of domestic appliances. Drawing and painting were done on prepared buffalo skins, and elaborately carved pipes were made for ceremonial use.

The Sioux were divided into kinship groups, with inheritance as a rule in the male line. The woman was autocrat of the home. Exogamy was strictly enforced in the clan, but marriage within the tribe or with related tribes was encouraged. The marriage was arranged by the parents, and polygyny was common where means would permit. Government consisted in chieftainship acquired by personal merit. The older men exercised considerable influence.

Ownership of land was vested in the group who occupied it. Food was shared in common, the procurer having special privileges. Huts, dogs, weapons, etc., were personal property, and such possessions were destroyed at the death of the owner to provide for his wants in the spirit-world.

Their religious conceptions were based upon a belief in "Wakanda" or "Manitou," an all-pervading spiritual entity, whose cult involved various shamanistic ceremonials consisting of dancing, chanting, feasting and fasting. Most distinctive of these was the sun-dance, practised by almost all the tribes of the plains except the Comanche. It was an annual festival in honour of the sun lasting four days, characterised in the later stages by personal torture.

The *Pawnee* tribes were probably of southern origin. They were more addicted to agriculture than the Sioux, raising crops of maize, pumpkins and squashes. The Pawnee type of hut was characteristic, consisting of a circular framework of poles or logs covered with bush, bark and earth. They were divided into kinship groups, distinguished by totems, and inheritance was in the male line. The tribes were divided into bands under a chief, whose office was hereditary in the male line and whose power was more absolute than usual among Indians. Their religious ceremonials were similar to but more elaborate than those of the Sioux, and were formerly distinguished by human sacrifices to the morning star at the annual corn-planting, the victim being usually a captive girl from a hostile tribe (Farrand).

Northern Tribes of the Eastern Woodlands.

These consist of *Algonquians* and *Iroquois*. The *Ojibwa*, the chief central Algonquian tribe, were a typical people of the woods. The northern branch were mild, harmless hunters, the southern led a sort of sedentary life part of the time; maize, pumpkins, and beans were cultivated, and wild rice collected; much of the food was obtained by hunting and fishing. They were hard, fighters and beat back the raids of the Iroquois on the east and of the Foxes on the south, and drove the Sioux before them out of the plains. They were organised in many exogamous clans; descent was patrilineal, though matrilineal in most of the other tribes. The clan system was totemic. There was a clan chief and generally a tribal chief as well, chosen from one clan in which the office was hereditary. His authority was rather indefinite. As regards the religion of this group "there was a firm belief in a cosmic mystery present throughout all Nature; it was called Manitou. It was natural to identify the Manitou with both animate and inanimate objects, and the impulse was strong to enter into personal relation with the mystic power. There was one personification of the cosmic mystery, it was into an animate being called the Great Manitou" (W. Jones).

The famous League of the *Iroquois* was formed between 1400 and 1450 A.D. Each of the five tribes remained independent in matters of local concern, but supreme authority was delegated to a council of elected

G

sachems. So successful was this confederacy that for centuries it enjoyed complete supremacy over its neighbours, until it controlled the country from Hudson Bay to North Carolina. The powerful Ojibwa at the east of Lake Superior checked their north-western expansion, and their own kindred, the Cherokee, stopped their progress southwards. The Hurons were practically wiped out by them. They lived in "long houses" of related families, over which a matron presided; they afford an exceedingly good example of mother-right. The clans (gens of Morgan), which were always exogamous, were organised into phratries, which were also originally exogamous, but this restriction has long since been removed except in the case of the clans. The phratries had no strictly governmental functions, and appear chiefly in religious ceremonies and games.

Tribes of the South-west.

These may be grouped into two classes according to their mode of living—pueblo and non-pueblo peoples. A "pueblo" is a village of a communal type consisting of houses of five or six storeys arranged along courts or passageways, each storey being a separate residence, often reached from the roof of the one below. The Pueblo Indians are muscular and capable of great endurance, being able to carry heavy burdens and walk and run for long distances. They are mild and peaceable in disposition, industrious, and intensely conservative in their customs. They depend mainly on agriculture, raising crops of corn, cotton, melons, beans, tobacco, peaches, etc. The men do spinning, weaving, and knitting, and make cotton and woollen garments. The women build and own the houses, grind the meal, prepare the food, and carry the water; in addition they make pottery which has become famous for its quality and decoration. Each pueblo village has a peace-chief or governor and councillors, and a war-chief. The clans are numerous and form the entire basis of their social and religious organisation. Marriage is monogamous, the children belonging to the mother's clan and the daughters inheriting her property. Private property in land is not recognised.

The Pueblo Indians are very religious, much of their time being spent in elaborate ceremonials which are very complex, sometimes lasting over a week. These are controlled by secret societies or priesthoods, of which there are several in each village. The purpose of the ceremonies is to obtain rain, the very existence of the Pueblo Indians being dependent on the crops, notably corn.

CENTRAL AMERICA.

The greater part of southern Central America is inhabited by the *Maya* race, a branch of which formerly extended on to the plateau of Mexico, and was known as the *Toltecs*. North and south of these latter were, and to some extent still are, the *Otomi*, *Tarasco*, *Misteca*, and *Zapoteca* peoples. A thousand years ago the western half of Northern Mexico was occupied by the *Nahua*, one tribe of whom, the *Aztecs*, pressed the aboriginal population of Southern Mexico before them, and established themselves on the plateau, where they founded the city of Mexico. The Toltecs disappeared as such, but their culture was assimilated by the ruder Aztecs; the descendants of the former are still to be found in Guatemala and Yucatan, and are now merged among their Maya kinsfolk. The remarkable culture that the Spaniards found in Mexico was due mainly to the intelligent and gifted Maya peoples; it was entirely indigenous, and owed nothing to the culture of the Pueblo Indians of New Mexico and Arizona, or to the civilisations of the Andean regions of South America. The Nahua or Nahuatlaca appear to have come originally from the far north.

SOUTH AMERICA.

Following Deniker the natives may be grouped according to the four great natural regions:—(1) the Cordillera of the Andes; (2) the plains of the Amazon and the Orinoco, with Guiana; (3) the table-lands of eastern and southern Brazil; (4) the Pampas of the southern part of the continent, with Tierra del Fuego.

The Cordillera of the Andes.

The ancient Andean civilisation was the highest expression of South American culture. The peoples of this region consist mainly of members of the Chibcha and Quichua linguistic families, with a certain number of unclassified tribes. The most powerful of the former group were the *Muyscas* of the Rio Magdalena valley, who were dominant in the north with an organised system of government on the Bogota table-land. They were surrounded by numerous kindred tribes, still in a condition of savagery. The rigid caste system of the Muyscas stifled their development, and they are now extinct.

The Quichua dialects are still spoken over the area of the ancient Inca empire, which was almost contiguous in the north with that of the Muyscas. Three distinct civilisations had grown up about three cultural centres: that of the *Yuncas* (whom Deniker is unable to classify) developed about Chimu (Trujillo of the present day); that of the *Aymaras*, a people of Quichuan stock, about Tiahuanaco on the southern shores of Lake Titicaca; and that of the *Quichuas* about Cuzco. Prior to the arrival of the Europeans, however, the first two had been absorbed by the third, and the whole area constituted the empire of the Incas, who were the dominant branch of the Quichuan nation. The very name " Inca " was afterwards restricted to the royal family. The Incas also conquered the Calchaquis, another Quichua-speaking race, the most numerous and highly civilised of the former inhabitants of Argentina. The Quichuas are fairly uniform physically; they are of low stature, 1·575-1·6m. (5ft. 2-3in.), thickset and very strong, with massive globular head, aquiline nose, and retreating forehead due to cranial deformation.

Among the unclassified Andean peoples mention must be made of the *Araucanians* (or *Mapu-che*) whose territory extended south of the Peruvian empire, and who held their own against the Incas and after them the Conquistadores. They were little organised in time of peace, and their tribal groups at the present day are mere territorial divisions, such as Picun-che (north-men), Huilli-che (south-men), Molu-che (west-men), Puen-che (pine-men, i.e., people of the central pine country). The Puel-che (east-men) of the eastern slopes of the Andes afterwards moved down the Rio Negro and encountered the Pampean Indians with whom they mingled. The Araucanians have now adopted the peaceful pursuits of agriculture and stock-breeding, and the process of assimilation, completed in the Chiloe and Chonos Archipelagoes, is likely to spread on the mainland.

Before dealing with the two next great divisions, which include the Amazonians and the peoples of eastern Brazil and of central South America, reference must be made to the race migrations which have taken place throughout this vast area. The two chief linguistic subdivisions of the Amazonians are the Carib and the Arawak, while the two main groups of East-Brazilians are the Tupi-Guarani (or Tupi), and the Ges (or Tapuya). The original home of the Arawaks was probably Bolivia, whence they spread east, north-east, and south-east, forming a uniform substratum over a large part of the north of South America; their progress was only stayed where they encountered the Caribs and Tupis. The Caribs originally inhabited the upper courses of the Tapajos and other rivers flowing northward into the lower Amazon, up which they moved to the mouth of the Amazon. The Tupis peopled the upper basin of the Paraguay, not far from the original Carib region; they moved downstream to the Rio de la Plata, turning northward at the mouth and skirting the whole coast of Brazil

till they reached the mouth of the Amazon,   There they
met with the Caribs whom they forced to turn north-
wards, while they themselves passed along the southern
bank of the Amazon, the Arawaks being on the northern.
Tupi tribes (Omaguas and Cocamas) even reached as far
west as the Putumayo and the Marañon.   The Caribs
pushed the Arawaks before them, ultimately prevailing
from the mouth of the Amazon to the Lago de
Maracaibo.   Their conquest of the Arawaks of the
Antilles was arrested at the Discovery.   The Ges peoples
lived in Brazil from the earliest times, but took no active
part in history.   It is possible that they once extended
all over Brazil from the Amazon watershed to the
Parana, but at the time of the Conquest they only
inhabited the hill country of the interior.

*The Plains of the Amazon and the Orinoco
with Guiana.*

The northern part of South America east of the
Cordilleras is peopled mainly by Caribs and Arawaks,
but about the head-waters of the Amazon and its
tributaries are tribes of the Miranha and Pano linguistic
families, and some unclassified peoples occur there and
in the basin of the Orinoco.

The northern *Caribs* are 1·594m. (5ft 2¾in.) in height
with a cephalic index of 81·3; those of the Xingu are
taller, 1·664m. (5ft. 5½in.), with a cephalic index of 79·6.
The Caribs were formerly cannibals, and most ferocious in
their methods of warfare especially towards the Arawaks.
The following ethnical characteristics of the Caribs may

be noted:—the use of the hammocks, painting of the body, practice of couvade (lying-in of the father after the birth of a child); the chief weapon under primitive conditions is the stone axe, but the northern Caribs use the blow-pipe and poisoned arrows which are unknown to the southerners, who use the bow and arrow. The *Bakaïri* of the upper Xingu are a typical primitive Carib tribe. They are hunters and fishers, and to some extent agriculturists as well. Their clothing is of the slightest, but they are fond of shell or seed necklaces; their huts are beehive-shaped; implements are personal property, but plantations belong to the community; chieftainship is hereditary from father to son or to sister's son. They have very little religion, and their remarkable mask-dances do not appear to have much ceremonial importance.

The difference between the northern and southern *Arawaks* is more pronounced than with the Caribs; those of Guiana and also of the Purus basin (western Brazil) are 1·55-1·59m. (5ft. 1-2½in.) in height, with a cephalic index of 83·4, while the Arawaks of the Xingu are taller, 1·64m. (5ft. 4½in.), and have a cephalic index of 78·2. The blow-pipe is used only by the upper Amazon tribes; garments are of fibre or bark-cloth, and ornaments of feathers and teeth; their implements are of wood and stone.

The *Pano* tribes are in a state of transformation, some having taken to trading and agriculture. The *Miranhas* are a primitive and warlike hunting people, distinguishable by their peculiar nose-ornament, large shell studs being inserted in the nostrils. Among the unclassified tribes of the Amazon head-waters, the *Zaparos* (or *Jeberos*) are remarkable on account of their shamanistic religion, and the *Jevaros* (or *Civaros*) for their practice of head-hunting, the scalps of their enemies being preserved and regarded as valuable trophies.

There are four main linguistic groups of peoples in Guiana:—*Warrau, Arawak, Wapiana* (including true Wapiana, Atorais and Amaripas), and *Carib* (including Carinya or true Carib, Ackawoi, Macusi, and Arecuna), who all belong to the same race. The coast tract is inhabited by Warraus and Arawaks, with scattered settlements of Carinya. The forest region is almost entirely inhabited by Ackawoi, with a few Carinya camps. The savanna region, beginning with the north towards the Orinoco, is peopled by various tribes:—Arecunas, Macusis, Wapianas, Tarumas (a tribe of unknown affinities, which came from the south), and an isolated tribe of Caribs.

The natives are all of small stature; the main characters are a protuberant stomach from excessive drinking of paiwari (an intoxicant made by chewing cassava bread), and sleekness and fulness of skin from eating cassava. The skin is of a red cinnamon colour, the hair straight, long and black, the features gentle. They are weak in constitution. Their habits are exceptionally cleanly. They are affectionate in domestic relations, and their women are well treated, and have considerable influence, but old people are not well treated.

The men are hunters, and the women cultivate cassava. The clothing of the men is a strip of cloth passed between the legs and fastened to a belt; that of the women, an apron of beads. The houses are built on piles in the swamps; in the forests they are usually rectangular, with a ridge-pole, and roofed with palm leaves. On the savannas, walls daubed with mud are added. Their weapons are the bow and arrow, and blow-pipe.

The father is the head of the household, and the chief authorities in a group are the headman and the peaiman (or medicine-man). Most tribes are polygynous, but the Caribs are mainly monogamous; the polygynous Warrau are also polyandrous. Marriage is mostly a matter of purchase, and the husband lives with, works for, and is subject to his father-in-law. Descent is reckoned through the mother. The custom of carefully tending the father on the birth of a child (couvade) prevails. Religion consists mainly in the propitiation of evil spirits by mediation of the peaiman.

Very scanty information exists on the natives of the West Indies. The peaceful Arawaks appear to have been the aboriginal inhabitants, the islands being invaded later by the piratical and slave-hunting Caribs. St. Vincent and Dominica were the principal rendezvous of the insular Caribs, although they occupied all the islands from Puerto Rico to the Orinoco, and raided at times Jamaica and San Domingo, but had no permanent villages north of Jamaica; a few still exist in St. Vincent and possibly elsewhere. The 'Yellow Caribs' must be distinguished from the 'Black Caribs' or Karifs, who are a Carib-Negro mixture.

Eastern and Southern Brazil.

Eastern Brazil is mainly occupied by peoples of the *Ges* family, formerly called *Tapuyas*. This region is poor in resources, and the people are generally more backward than the Amazonians. Ethnical characteristics common to these tribes are:—communal houses with separate hearths for the various families, absence of the hammock, ignorance of navigation, wearing of plugs (botoques) in the lower lip or ears, arrows barbed on one side. The best known element in this group is the *Botocudo* people. They are nomad hunters and collectors, with implements of wood and vegetable fibre, living in flimsy huts of branches. They go nude, and wear the teeth of those they have eaten strung on necklaces. They are cannibals, eating both enemies and fellow tribesmen. Their women are brutally treated. They are of low stature, 1·59m. (5ft. 2½in.), and have relatively narrow heads, their cephalic index varying from about 76 to 78. Many of the Brazilian tribes have dwindled to a few individuals living under the protection of the white man.

Tupi tribes speaking various dialects occur in different parts from Guiana to Paraguay, and from the coast of Brazil to the Cordilleras. At the time of the Conquest they were cannibals occupying the Atlantic coast from the Para to 24° south latitude, and the Amazon valley up to 60° west longitude. They were largely exterminated by the Portuguese, but their language became the means of communicating with the Indians of Brazil and Paraguay.

The eastern, or *Guarani Tupis*, formerly very numerous in South Brazil, now form a considerable proportion of the population of Paraguay and Missiones (Argentina). Those of Paraguay have become largely hispanified. Some forest tribes retain the real type, such for instance as the *Cainguas* or *Kaigguas*, who are scattered about in small groups over the southern part of the region mentioned. They are short (5ft. 3in.), with a cephalic index of 80·4, bronzed skin, lank or wavy hair, and prominent cheekbones. They go almost nude; fire is obtained by friction; they are agriculturists, weavers and potters. Other members of the eastern Tupi group are the Tacunas and Jacunda of the lower Xingu, the Kamayuras of the upper Xingu, the Mauhés between that river and the Madeira, the Apiacas of the Tapajos, and the Chiquitos and Chiriguanos of Bolivia; the last two are now largely hispanified.

The western Tupis comprise the Mundurukus of the middle Tapajos, and the Yurunas and Auetö of the Xingu. The *Mundurukus* are head-hunters of extreme ferocity in warfare; the rank of chief is attained by the capture of at least ten heads. Youths go through an initiation ceremony in the form of a glove-dance; the bachelors live in separate huts.

In addition to Caribs, Arawaks, Ges, and Tupis, there are representatives of other ethnic groups to be met with in Matto Grosso and south-eastern Bolivia. The more important of these are the *Karayas*, of whom there are two sections knowing nothing of each other, one in the Xingu valley, the other in that of the Araguaya. They are of medium height, and narrow head (cephalic index 73).

They do not use hammocks, are good navigators, and the
women speak a different language from the men, apparently an older form. The *Trumai* of the upper Xingu
are short, with medium heads (cephalic index 81·1),
retreating forehead and convex nose. The *Bororos* are
scattered from the upper Paraguay to the upper Parana.
They are tall, 1·74m. (5ft. 8½in.), with a cephalic index
of 81·5. They are a purely hunting and collecting people,
who never practise agriculture, nor have they domestic
animals. They do not use canoes. The women wear a
broad tight belt and perineal band, the men a narrow
belt. They are very fond of feather decorations; both
sexes pierce the lobe of the ear, and the men bore the
lower lip. The men live in a clubhouse, and do not settle
down and marry till they are about forty, when they live
in very poor huts. They sometimes capture women and
take them to the clubhouse. The married men arrange
the affairs of the community, and a chief commands in
war. The dead are temporarily buried, and later there
is a special funeral ceremony. The souls of the dead are
believed to enter the bodies of birds.

The Pampas of the South, with Tierra del Fuego.

This division comprises the great plain beyond 30°
south latitude, which passes from the rich pasturage of
Gran Chaco to Pampas, and then to the bare plateaus of
Patagonia. The inhabitants of the plain are nomadic
and pastoral in their way of life since the introduction of
the horse. Only hybridised descendants remain of the
ancient peoples who lived here and in Uruguay at the time

of the Conquest, such as the Talhuets and Abipones, who represent some of the old members of the Guaycuru family. This family still survives in its pure form in some Chaco tribes, such as the Tobas, Matacos, and Payaguas; others, such as the Lenguas, Sanapanas, and Angaites, belong to the Ennema linguistic family. South of the Chaco, in the Pampas and the north Patagonian tableland, the Guaycurus of the north, and the Patagonians of the south, have been absorbed or modified by the Araucanians from the west, and the Europeans from the east. New tribes have thus arisen, such as the Puel-che from Patagonians, and Araucanians with a Guaycuru strain, and Gauchos from Guaycurus and Europeans. To avoid confusion it must be noted that the term Puel-che (east-men) was applied first to the pure Araucanians of the east side of the Andes, and then to the Pampeans, and is still used indiscriminately for the pure Araucanians of the Argentine Republic, Pampeans, and nomads generally as far south as the Rio Negro.

The Europeans gradually pushed the Puel-che and Araucanians southward, the Pampeans migrating *en masse* in 1881 beyond the Rio Negro, where they mingled with some of the Patagonians and drove the rest beyond the Rio Santa Cruz. Some two thousand *Patagonians*, or *Tehuel-che*, now live between this river and the Strait of Magellan. Those inland and the Onas of Tierra del Fuego best preserve the Patagonian type. They are very tall, 1·73-1·83m. (5ft. 8in. or 6ft.), according to different accounts, with a cephalic index of 85,

PATAGONIANS.

Plate X.]   [Races of Man, p. 100.

elongated face, slightly oblique eyes, prominent cheek bones, black lank hair, and dark coppery complexion· They subsist mainly on the flesh of the guanaco and other wild animals; horse-flesh is also used by some; a few wild vegetables are eaten, but nothing is cultivated· They are a well-clothed people, not even the children go nude; silver ornaments are worn. Their dwellings are leather tents or brushwood huts, and characteristic weapons are lassos and bolas. They are divided into a number of independent clans, each with its hereditary chief with somewhat restricted power. They believe in demons, over which medicine-men are supposed to have power. The dead were till recently buried in a sitting posture, and weapons were also put in the grave.

The *Fuegians* inhabit the south and west of Tierra del Fuego and the off-lying archipelagoes. They consist of two tribes, the *Yahgans* and the *Alakalufs*, of whom the former are probably the true aborigines and may be taken as typical of the Fuegians. They are of low stature, with a large head, angular face, short nose depressed at root and wide at nostrils, large thick lips, and small black eyes often obliquely set. Their food consists mainly of mussels and animal food, but berries are eaten in summer and roots in winter. They were said formerly to eat their old women. They have no kitchen utensils nor pottery. As clothing they wear a small piece of skin over the shoulders, and the women have in addition a very short narrow apron. Their dwellings are flimsy huts, made of logs and branches. Hunting is undertaken by the men and fishing by the women. They make perishable bark canoes. Monogamy is the general rule. They do not recognise virtue, but they do not practise vice. Modesty is strongly developed; compassion is almost unknown. They are courageous, vain, and susceptible. Lying is no evil, but the murderer is banned by all.

BIBLIOGRAPHY

———∞○∞○∞———

This Bibliography is intended merely as a guide to the elementary student, and only those books are included which have reference to my immediate object, as further references to other books or to memoirs and papers will be found in them. As this little book is designed to help the beginner in ethnology, very few references are made to works in other languages. The Journal of the Royal Anthropological Institute is a mine of information, as are the journals of kindred foreign societies. The numerous books by travellers and missionaries, which deal with special areas and peoples, should also be consulted.

THE GENERAL SUBJECT.

Deniker, J.—"The Races of Man," 1900.

Duckworth, W. L. H. — "Morphology and Anthropology," 1904.

Haddon, A. C.—"The Study of Man," 1898.

Keane, A. H.—"Ethnology," 1901; "Man: Past and Present," 1905; "The World's Peoples," 1908.

Ratzel, F.—"The History of Mankind" (translation), 1896-8.

Reclus, J. J. E.—"The Earth and its Inhabitants" (translation), 1875.

Ripley, W. Z.—"The Races of Europe," 1900.

Topinard, P.—"Anthropology" (translation), 1890.

Tylor, E. B.—"Anthropology," 1895.

H

Wiedersheim, R.—"The Structure of Man" (translation), 1895.

Wood, J. G.—"The Natural History of Man."

Other books that should be consulted are:—"The World's History," *editor*, Helmolt, H. F. (various volumes); "Stanford's Compendium of Geography and Travel" (various volumes); "The Living Races of Mankind."

OCEANIA.

Australians.

Curr, E. M.—"The Australian Race," 1886-87.

Gennep, A. Van.—"Mythes et Légendes d'Australie: études d'Ethnographie et de Sociologie," 1906.

Howitt, A. W.—"The Native Tribes of South-east Australia," 1904.

Mathew, J.—"Eaglehawk and Crow," 1899.

Roth, W. E.—"Bulletins of North Queensland Ethnography," 1901.

Smyth, R. B.—"The Aborigines of Victoria," 1878.

Spencer, B., and Gillen, F. J.—"The Native Tribes of Central Australia," 1899; "The Northern Tribes of Central Australia," 1904.

Thomas, N. W.—"Natives of Australia," 1906; "Kinship Organisation, etc., in Australia," 1906.

Papuans and Melanesians.

Codrington, R. H.—"The Melanesians," 1891.

Guppy, H. B.—"The Solomon Islands," 1887.

Haddon, A. C.—"Head-hunters," 1901; "Reports Cambridge Expedition to Torres Straits."

Parkinson, R.—"Dreissig Jahre in der Sudsee," 1907.

Roth, H. L.—"The Aborigines of Tasmania," 1889.

Sande, G. A. J. van der—"Nova Guinea, III. Ethnography and Anthropology," 1907.

Thomson, B.—"The Fijians," 1908.

Thomson, J. P.—" British New Guinea," 1892.

Williams, T. and Calvert, J.—" Fiji and the Fijians," 1858.

Polynesians.

Ellis, W.—" Polynesian Researches, etc.," 1831.

Fornander, A.—"An Account of the Polynesian Race," 1878-85.

Gill, W. W.—"Myths and Songs from the South Pacific," 1876.

Grey, G.—" Polynesian Mythology," 1853.

Lesson, P. A.—" Les Polynésiens," 1880-84,

Mariner, W.—"An Account of the Natives of the Tonga Islands," 1818.

Smith, S. P.—" Hawaiki," 1904.

Taylor, R.—"Te Ika a Maui," 1855.

Turner, G.—" Nineteen Years in Polynesia," 1861 ; " Samoa," 1884.

AFRICA.

Negrilloes.

Johnston, H. H.—" The Uganda Protectorate," 1902.

Stanley, H. M.—" In Darkest Africa," 1890.

Bushmen and Hottentots.

Stow, G. W.—"The Native Races of South Africa," 1905.

Theal, C. M'C.—" History and Ethnography of South Africa," 1907.

Bantus.

Callaway, H.—" Nursery Tales, etc,," 1868 ; " The Religious System of the Amazulu," 1870.

Casati, G.—" Ten Years in Equatoria " (translation), 1891.

Cassalis, E.—" The Basutos " (translation), 1861.

Johnston, H. H. (l.c.)

Junod, H. A.—"Les Ba-Ronga," 1898.

Kidd, D.—"The Essential Kafir," 1904; "Savage Childhood," 1906; " Kafir Socialism." 1908.

Macdonald, D.—"Africana," 1882.

Stow (l.c.), Theal (l.c.)

Werner, A.—"The Natives of British Central Africa," 1906.

Negroes.

Dennett, R. E.—"At the Back of the Black Man's Mind," 1906.

Ellis, A. B.—"The Tshi-speaking Peoples," 1887; "The Ewe," 1890; "The Yoruba," 1894.

Johnston, H. H.—"Liberia," 1906.

Kingsley, M.—"West African Studies," 1901.

Leonard, A. G.—"The Lower Niger," 1906.

Nassau, R. H.—"Fetichism in West Africa," 1904.

Various African Tribes.

Dowd, J.—"The Negro Races," 1907.

Fritsch, G.—"Die Eingeborenen Süd-Afrika's," 1872.

Hartmann, R.—"Die Nigritier," 1876.

Hollis, A. C.—"The Masai," 1905; "The Nandi," 1909.

Johnston—"The Uganda Protectorate," 1902.

Klunzinger, C. B.—"Upper Egypt" (translation), 1878.

Preville, A.de—"Les Sociétés Africaines," 1894.

EUROPE.

Beddoe, J.—"The Races of Britain," 1885.

Borlase, W. C.—"The Dolmens of Ireland," 1897.

Deniker, J.—"Les Races de l'Europe, I. l'Indice céphalique," 1899; Association Française Avance, Sci. (1897).

Fouillée, A.—"Esquisse psychologique des Peuples Européens," 1903.

Holmes, T. Rice—"Ancient Britain," 1907.

Mackinder, H. J.—"The Racial and Historical Geography of Britain," 1902.

Rhys, J.—"Celtic Britain," 1904.

Ripley, W. Z.—"The Races of Europe," 1900.

Sergi, G.—"The Mediterranean Race," 1901.

ASIA.

Hogarth, D. G.—"The Nearer East," 1902.

Jackson, F. G.—"The Great Frozen Land," 1895.

Little, A.—"The Farther East."

Stanford's "Compendium of Geography."

"The Jesup North Pacific Expedition." Mem. Am. Mus. Nat. Hist. Various memoirs by Bogoras, W., and Jochelson, W.

INDIA.

Biddulph, J.—"Tribes of the Hindu-Kush," 1880.

Crooke, W.—"The Tribes and Castes of the North-west Provinces and Oudh," 1896; "The North-west Provinces of India," 1897; "Natives of India." 1907.

Dalton, E. T.—" Descriptive Ethnology of Bengal," 1872.

Dubois, J. A.—"Hindu Manners, etc.," (translation), 1897.

Gait, E. A.—" A History of Assam," 1906.

Gurdon, P. R. T.—"The Khasis," 1907.

Hodson, T. C.—"The Meitheis," 1908.

Holdich, T. A.—" India," 1904.

Hunter, W.W.—"A Statistical Account of Assam," 1879.

Kennedy, J.—"The Mediæval History of Northern India"; cf. "The Indian Empire," vol. II.

Man, E. H.—"Aboriginal Inhabitants of the Andaman Islands," Journal Anth. Inst. XII., 1882.

Marshall, W. E.—"A Phrenologist among the Todas," 1873.

Oppert, G.—"The Original Inhabitants of India," 1894.

Powell, B. H. Baden—"The Indian Village Community," 1896.

Risley, H. H.—"The Tribes and Castes of Bengal, etc.," 1892; "The People of India," 1908.

Rivers, W. H. R.—"The Todas," 1906.

Robertson, G. S.—"The Kafirs of the Hindu-Kush," 1896.

Smith, V. A.—"The early History of India," 1908.

Stack, E.—"The Mikirs," 1908.

Thurston, E.—"Ethnographical Notes in Southern India," 1906.

Ujfalvy, C. de.—"Les Aryens au Nord et au Sud de l'Hindou-Kouch," 1896.

See also "The Indian Empire" (4 vols.), being the introduction to "The Imperial Gazetteer of India," new edition, 1907; "Census of India," "Bulletin of the Madras Museum," "Journal of the Asiatic Society of Bengal," etc.

THE MALAY PENINSULA AND BURMA.

Forbes, C. J. F. S.—" British Burma and its People," 1878.

Hall, H. F.—" The Soul of a People," 1898; "A People at School," 1906.

Martin, R.—" Die Inlandstämme der Malayischen Halbinsel," 1905.

Moszkowski, M.—" Zeitschrift für Ethnologie, XL," 1908, pp. 229, 634.

Scott, J. G.—" The Burman," 1896; " Burma," 1906.

Skeat, W. W.—" Malay Magic," 1900; and Blagden, C. O.—" Pagan Races of the Malay Peninsula," 1906.

Swettenham, F. A.—" The Real Malay," 1900.

Wilkinson, R. J.—" The Peninsula Malays," 1906.

BORNEO.

Furness, W. H.—" The Home Life of the Borneo Head-Hunters," 1902.

Haddon, A. C.—" Head-Hunters," 1901.

Nieuwenhuis, A. W.—" Quer durch Borneo," 1904-07.

Roth, H. L.—" The Natives of Sarawak," 1896.

CHINA AND JAPAN.

Bard, E.—" The Chinese at Home."

Batchelor, G.—" The Ainu of Japan," 1892.

Brinkley, F.—" Japan : Its History, Arts, and Literature " (Oriental Series), 1901.

Carles, W.—" Life in Corea," 1888.

Chamberlain, B.—" Things Japanese," 1891.

Hearn, Lafcadio—" Japan : an Interpretation," 1904.

" History of the Empire of Japan " (various authors), 1893.

Lacouperie, Terrien de—"The Languages of China before the Chinese," 1887 ; "Western origin of the early Chinese civilization," 1894.

Okakura, Y.—"The Japanese Spirit," 1905.

Richthofen—"China" vol. I, 1875.

Rockhill, W. W.—"Notes on the Ethnology of Tibet," 1895.

Smith, A. H.—"Chinese Characteristics," 1895.

NORTH AMERICA.

Bancroft, H. H.—"The Native Races of the Pacific States," 1874-82.

Boas, F.—"Social Organization of the Kwakiutl," U.S. Nat. Mus. Report, 1895; "North-western Tribes of Canada," Brit. Assoc. Report, 1898.

Boyle, D. (and others).—"Ethnography of Canada," Arch. Report, Ontario, 1905 (with many references to bibliography).

Brinton, D. G.—"The American Race," 1891.

Farrand, L.—"Basis of American History," 1904.

Hill-Tout, C.—"British North America," 1907.

Hodge, F. W. (and others).—"Handbook of American Indians north of Mexico," 1907.

Maclean, J.—"The Indians." 1892; "Canadian Savage Folk," 1896.

Nansen, F.—"Eskimo Life," 1893.

Rink, H. J.—"Tales and Traditions of the Eskimo," 1875.

Whymper, F.—"Travels in Alaska," 1868.

"The American Anthropologist" and "The Journal of American Folk-Lore."

"The Annual Report of the Director of the Bureau of American Ethnology," 1881, etc.

" The Jesup North Pacific Expedition," Mem. Am. Mus. Nat. Hist., various vols.

University of California Publications in American Archæology and Ethnology.

Field Columbian Museum (Field Museum of Natural History) Publications, Anthropological Series, Chicago.

CENTRAL AND SOUTH AMERICA.

Brett, W. H.—" The Indian Tribes of Guiana," 1868.

Dance, C. D.—" Chapters from a Guianese Log-Book," 1881.

Gadow, H.—" Through Southern Mexico," 1908.

Hyades, P., et Deniker, J.—" Mission scientifique du Cap Horn," 1891.

Im Thurn, E. F.—"Among the Indians of Guiana," 1883.

Keane, A. H.—" Central America and the West Indies," 1901 ; " South America," 1901.

Lumholtz, C.—" Unknown Mexico," 1902.

Payne, E. J.—" History of the New World called America," 1892, 1899.

Steinen, K. von den.—" Unter den Naturvolkern Zentral-Brasiliens," 1894

GLOSSARY.

Animal helper : An animal seen by a young man in a trance, which was supposed to be a manifestation of spiritual power, and thereafter helped him throughout life.

Animatism (Marett) is a stage antecedent to animism, in which even material objects are endowed with life, or are regarded as living because of their own proper powers, or because they are self-power.

Animism is the conception of a spirit energising objects, more especially of "souls of individual creatures, capable of continued existence after death or the destruction of the body," and of "other spirits, upward to the rank of powerful deities" (Tylor).

Anthropophagy : Man-eating, cannibalism.

Brachycephalic : Broad-headed, having a cranial or cephalic index exceeding 80.

Caste : A section of a larger community which stands in definite relations to other similar sections, and which usually has an occupational basis and a definite rule of endogamy.

Caucasic : A term applied by some authors to Europeans and to other peoples possessing more or less similar physical characters.

Cephalic index : The ratio of the breadth to the length in the head of a living subject, the length being taken as 100.

Cheloid : A raised scar.

Clan : See *sept.*

Class : (Australia) A division of a phratry.

Classificatory system of relationship : A system of relationship under which relatives are grouped mainly according to age-status and sex; for example, a mother's sister, mother's brother's wife, father's brother's wife, and other women of that generation, are called by the same term as the actual mother.

Communal houses : Large houses shared by a community, such as a totem-sept or village group.

Couvade : A widely spread custom, which requires the father to rest or be in seclusion immediately after the birth of a child. This custom appears to be the logical outcome of a more or less rigid series of food or action taboos which are enforced previous to the birth of the child, and which may be continued afterwards.

Cranial index : The ratio of the breadth to the length in the skull, the length being taken as 100.

Cymotrichi : People having wavy or curly hair. Adj. cymotrichous.

Dolichocephalic : Narrow-headed, having a cranial or cephalic index below 75.

Endogamy : The obligation to marry within the group.

Exogamy : The obligation to marry outside the group.

Family : This term should be limited to the group of parents and children. The "extended family" is a group of persons descended from the same grandfather or grandmother, or more distant progenitor (actual, and not mythical, as is often the case in the sept). Occasionally, the extended family and the sept may correspond with one another.

Father-right : A state of society in which descent is reckoned through the father; the wife, on marriage, usually goes to live permanently with the husband's family or group; authority in the family is in the father's hands.

Fetish : Any object credited with mysterious powers owing to its having personality and will, or to its being, even temporarily, the representative or habitation of a spirit or deity.

Frizzly : See *ulotrichous.*

Leiotrichi : People having straight, lank hair. Adj. leiotrichous.

Leptorrhine : Having a nose narrow at the wings.

Local group : A community, totemic or otherwise, living in an area over which it has collecting, hunting, and other rights.

Mana : Described on p. 27.

Manitou : Described on p. 87.

Matrilineal : Where descent is reckoned through the mother.

Mesaticephalic : Medium-headed, having a cranial or cephalic index between 75 and 80.

Mesorrhine : With a nose of moderate breadth at the wings.

Moiety : When there are only two phratries, and they are exogamous, so that a member of one division must marry a member of the other, the divisions are sometimes termed moieties.

Mongolian eye : The eye is typically oblique, and shaped like a scalene triangle; there is also a puffiness of the upper eyelid, which turns down at the inner angle of the narrowed eye, and instead of being free, as in the ordinary eye, is folded towards the eyeball, forming a fixed fold in front of the movable ciliary edge; this last becomes invisible, and the eyelashes are scarcely seen; also towards the inner angle of the eye, the eyelid forms a fold covering more or less of the caruncula, and may extend below it. (cf. Deniker).

Monogamy: The marriage of one male with one female.

Mother-right: A state of society in which there are two or all of the three conditions: (1) descent is reckoned through the mother; (2) on marriage the husband goes to live with the wife; (3) authority in the family is in the hands of the mother, the maternal uncles, or the mother's relatives in general.

Nation: A complex group which may consist of various tribes or groups, speaking different languages, but united under a common government for external affairs. The constituents of a nation usually, however, speak the same language. Cf. p. 6.

Orthognathous: Having no projection of the lower part of the face.

Patrilineal: Where descent is reckoned through the father.

People: A community inhabiting any given area independent of race. Cf. p. 6.

Perineal band: A band passing between the legs, fastened to a string round the hips.

Phratry: A division of a tribe or local community which usually includes two or more exogamous septs or clans.

Platyrrhine: Having a nose broad at the wings.

Polyandry: Marriage of one female with two or more males.

Polygamy: Combined polygynous and polyandrous marriage.

Polygyny: Marriage of one male with two or more females.

Prognathous: Having the lower part of the face projecting.

Pueblo: Village; for Pueblo Indians, see p. 88.

Pygmy: Applied to those people whose average stature falls below 1·5m. (4ft. 11in.).

Race: A main division of mankind, the members of which have important physical characters in common.

Sachem: A "peace-chief" who regulates the ordinary affairs of the community, but does not lead a war-party.

Scarification: Marking the skin with definite scars, a common practice of dark-skinned people, such scars being lighter in colour than the original skin.

Sept: The smallest exogamous section of a tribe or local community.

Shamanism: A cult based on conceptions similar to those of fetishism, the sorcerer, or animistic priest, being frequently termed a *Shaman*.

Steatopygia: A large development of fatty tissue in the buttocks.

Sulia: Described on p. 83; also cf. *Manitou*.

Supernatural helpers: cf. *Animal helpers*.

Taboo (tabu): A Polynesian word implying separated or set apart either as forbidden or as sacred; placed under ban or prohibition; consecrated either to avoidance or to special use or regard. Cf. p. 30.

Tattooing (tatuing): Puncturing designs in the skin by means of a sharp pointed instrument which drives pigment below the surface of the skin.

Territorial exogamous group: A group of people who must marry out of their district.

Totemism: A mystical connection uniting certain individuals with a class of natural objects, usually all the members of a species of animal or a plant; sometimes the *totem* is an inanimate body. Such group is best termed a *totem-sept*, but it has more frequently been termed a totem-clan, totem-kin, or totem-gens.

Frequently there is practical reciprocity between the totem and the human members of the totem-sept. All individuals having the same totem, even when belonging to different local communities or tribes, are regarded as brethren; thus all septs, of whatever locality, having the same totem are virtually one sept. Typically each totem-sept is exogamous. Frequently totem-septs are grouped into phratries. Often the members of a totem-sept are supposed to influence the totem for the good of the community, and they may not injure or eat it under ordinary circumstances; there is thus a reciprocity between them. All human beings having the same totem must help and never injure one another.

Tribe: A group of a simple kind occupying a circumscribed area, having a common language, common government, and a common action in warfare. Cf. p. 6.

Ulotrichi: People having hair with numerous, close, curly, often interlocking spirals. Adj. ulotrichous.

Wakanda: Described on p. 86.

INDEX

The darker figures are the chief references.

MILNER AND COMPANY, LIMITED, PRINTERS, HALIFAX.

www.ingramcontent.com/pod-product-compliance
Ingram Content Group UK Ltd.
Pitfield, Milton Keynes, MK11 3LW, UK
UKHW042152280225
455719UK00001B/285